A Solemn Appeal

by

Ellen G. White

TEACH Services, Inc.
www.TEACHServices.com

Copyright © 1996, 2011 TEACH Services, Inc.
ISBN-13: 978-1-57258-100-5
Library of Congress Control Number: 96-60001

Published by
TEACH Services, Inc.
www.TEACHServices.com

Table of Contents

Chapter 1

Appeal to Mothers

My Sisters: My apology for addressing you on this subject is, I am a mother, and feel alarmed for those children and youth who by solitary vice are ruining themselves for this world, and for that which is to come. Let us closely inquire into this subject from a physical, mental, and moral point of view.

Mothers, let us first view the results of this vice upon the physical strength. Have you not marked the lack of healthful beauty, of strength and power of endurance, in your dear children? Have you not felt saddened as you have watched the progress of disease upon them, which has baffled your skill, and that of physicians? You listen to numerous complaints of headache, catarrh, dizziness, nervousness, pain in the shoulders and side, loss of appetite, pain in the back and limbs, wakeful, feverish nights, of tired feelings in the morning, and great exhaustion after exercising? As you have seen the beauty of health disappearing, and have marked the sallow countenance, or the unnaturally-flushed face, have you been aroused sufficiently to look beneath the surface, to inquire into the cause of this physical decay? Have you observed the astonishing mortality among the

1

youth?

And have you not noticed that there was a deficiency in the mental health of your children? that their course seemed to be marked with extremes? that they were absent minded? that they started nervously when spoken to? and were easily irritated? Have you not noticed that, when occupied upon a piece of work, they would look dreamingly, as though the mind was elsewhere? and when they came to their senses, they were unwilling to own the work as coming from their hands, it was so full of mistakes, and showed such marks of inattention? Have you not been astonished at their wonderful forgetfulness? The most simple and oft-repeated directions would often be forgotten. They might be quick to learn, but it would be of no special benefit to them. The mind would not retain it. What they might learn through hard study, when they would use their knowledge, is missing, lost through their sieve-like memories. Have you not noticed their reluctance to engage in active labor? and their unwillingness to perseveringly accomplish that which they have undertaken which taxes the mental, as well as the physical, strength? The tendency of many is to live in indolence.

Have you not witnessed the gloomy sadness upon the countenance, and frequent exhibitions of a morose temper in those who once were cheerful, kind, and affectionate? They are easily excited to jealousy, disposed to look upon the dark side, and when you are laboring for their good, imagine that you are their enemy, that you needlessly reprove and restrain them.

And have you not inquired where will all this end, as you

have looked upon your children from a moral point of view? Have you not noticed the increase of disobedience in children, and their manifestations of ingratitude and impatience under restraint? Have you not been alarmed at their disregard of parental authority, which has bowed down the hearts of their parents with grief, and prematurely sprinkled their heads with gray hairs? Have you not witnessed the lack of that noble frankness in your children which they once possessed, and which you admired in them? Some children even express in their countenances a hardened look of depravity. Have you not felt distressed and anxious as you have seen the strong desire in your children to be with the other sex, and the overpowering disposition they possessed to form attachments when quite young? With your daughters, the boys have been the theme of conversation; and with your sons, it has been the girls. They manifest preference for particular ones, and your advice and warnings produce but little change. Blind passion overrules sensible considerations. And, although you may check the outward manifestations, and you credit the promises of amendment, yet, to your sorrow, you find there is no change, only to conceal the matter from you. There are still secret attachments and stolen interviews. They follow their willful course, and are controlled by their passions, until you are startled by perhaps a premature marriage, or are brought to shame by those who should, by their noble course of conduct, bring to you respect and honor. The cases of premature marriage multiply. Boys and girls enter upon the marriage relation with unripe love, immature judgment, without noble, elevated feelings, and take upon themselves the marriage vows, wholly led by their boyish, girlish passions. They choose for themselves, often without the knowledge of the mother who has watched over them, and cared for them, from their earliest infancy.

Attachments formed in childhood have often resulted in a very wretched union, or in a disgraceful separation. Early connections, if formed without the consent of parents, have seldom proved happy. The young affections should be restrained until the period arrives when sufficient age and experience will make it honorable and safe to unfetter them. Those who will not be restrained, will be in danger of dragging out an unhappy existence. A youth not out of his teens is a poor judge of the fitness of a person, as young as himself, to be his companion for life. After their judgment has become more matured, they view themselves bound for life to each other, and perhaps not at all calculated to make each other happy. Then, instead of making the best of their lot, recriminations take place, the breach widens, until there is settled indifference and neglect of each other. To them there is nothing sacred in the word home. The very atmosphere is poisoned by unloving words and bitter reproaches. The offspring of such are placed in a much more unfavorable condition than were their parents. With such surroundings, such examples, what could be expected of them if time should continue? Mothers, the great cause of these physical, mental, and moral evils, is secret vice, which inflames the passions, fevers the imagination, and leads to fornication and adultery. This vice is laying waste the constitution of very many, and preparing them for diseases of almost every description. And shall we permit our children to pursue a course of self-destruction?

Mothers, view your children from a religious standpoint. It gives you pain to see your children feeble in body and mind; but does it not cause you still greater grief to see them almost dead to spiritual things, so that they have but little desire for goodness, beauty of character, and holy purposes? Secret vice is the destroyer of high resolve, earnest endeavor, and strength of will to form a good religious character. All who have any true sense of what is embraced in being a Christian, know that the followers of Christ are under obligation as his disciples, to bring all their passions, their physical powers and mental faculties, into perfect subordination to his will. Those who are controlled by their passions cannot be followers of Christ. They are too much devoted to the service of their master, the originator of every evil, to leave their corrupt habits, and choose the service of Christ.

Godly mothers will inquire, with the deepest concern, Will our children continue to practice habits which will unfit them for any responsible position in this life? Will they sacrifice comeliness, health, intellect, and all hope of Heaven, everything worth possessing, here and hereafter, to the demon passion? May God grant that it may be otherwise; and that our children, who are so dear to us, may listen to the voice of warning, and choose the path of purity and holiness.

How important that we teach our children self-control from their very infancy, and teach them the lesson of submitting their wills to ours. If they should be so unfortunate as to learn wrong habits, not knowing all the evil results, they can be reformed by appealing to their reason, and convincing them that such habits ruin the constitution, and affect the mind. We should show them that whatever persuasions corrupt persons may use to quiet their awakened fears, and lead them still to indulge this pernicious habit, whatever may be their pretense, they are really their enemies and the devil's agents. Virtue and purity are of great value. These precious traits are of heavenly origin. They make God our friend, and unite us firmly to his throne.

Satan is controlling the minds of the young, and we must work resolutely and faithfully to save them. Very young children practice this vice, and it grows upon them and strengthens with their years, until every noble faculty of body and mind is debased. Many might have been saved if they had been carefully instructed in regard to the influence of this practice upon their health. They were ignorant of the fact that they were bringing much suffering upon themselves. Children who are experienced in this vice, seem to be bewitched by the devil until they can impart their vile knowledge to others, even teaching very young children this practice.

Mothers, you cannot be too careful in preventing your children from learning low habits. It is easier to guard them from evil, than for them to eradicate it after it is learned. Neighbors may permit their children to come to your house, to spend the evening and the night with your children. Here is a trial, and a choice for you, to run the risk of offending your neighbors by sending their children to their own home, or gratify them, and let them lodge with your children, and thus expose them to be instructed in that knowledge which would be a life-long curse to them.

To save my children from being corrupted, I have not allowed them to sleep in the same bed, nor in the same room, with other boys, and have, as occasion has required, when traveling, made a scanty bed upon the floor for them, rather than have them lodge with others. I have tried to keep them from associating with rough, rude boys, and have presented inducements before them to make their employment at home cheerful and happy. By keeping their minds and hands occupied, they have had but little time, or disposition, to play in the street with other boys, and obtain a street education.

A misfortune, which occurred when I was about nine years old, ruined my health. I looked upon this as a great calamity, and murmured because of it. In a few years I viewed the matter quite differently. I then looked upon it in the light of a blessing. I regard it thus now. Because of sickness, I was kept from society, which preserved me in blissful ignorance of the secret vices of the young. After I was a mother, by the private death-bed confessions of some females, who had completed the work of ruin, I first learned that such vices existed. But I had no just conception of the extent of this vice, and the injury the health sustained by it, until a still later period.

The young indulge to quite an extent in this vice before the age of puberty, without experiencing at that time, to any very great degree, the evil results upon the constitution. But at this critical period, while merging into manhood and womanhood, nature then makes them feel the previous violation of her laws.

As the mother sees her daughter languid and dispirited, with but little vigor, easily irritated, starting suddenly and nervously when spoken to, she feels alarmed, and fears that she will not be able to reach womanhood with a good constitution. She relieves her, if possible, from active labor, and anxiously consults a physician, who prescribes for her without making searching inquiries, or suggesting to the unsuspecting mother the probable cause of her daughter's illness. Secret indulgence is, in many cases, the only real cause of the numerous complaints of the young. This vice is laying waste the vital forces, and debilitating the system; and until the habit, which produced the result, is broken off, there can be no permanent cure. To relieve the young from healthful labor, is the worst possible course a parent can pursue. Their life is then aimless, the mind and hands unoccupied, the imagination active, and left free to indulge in thoughts that are not pure and healthful. In this condition they are inclined to indulge still more freely in that vice which is the foundation of all their complaints.

Mothers, it is a crime for you to allow yourselves to remain in ignorance in regard to the habits of your children. If they are pure, keep them so. Fortify their young minds, and prepare them to detest this health and soul destroying vice. Shield them, as faithful mothers should, from becoming contaminated by associating with every young companion. Keep them, as precious jewels, from the corrupting influence of this age. If you are situated so that their intercourse with young associates cannot always be overruled, as you would wish to have it, then let them visit your children in your presence, and in no case allow these associates to lodge in the same bed, or even in the same room. It will be far easier to prevent an evil than to cure it afterward.

If your children practice this vice, they may be in danger of resorting to falsehood to deceive you. But, mothers, you must not be easily quieted, and cease your investigations. You should not let the matter rest until you are fully satisfied. The health and souls of those you love are in peril, which makes this matter of the greatest importance. Determined watchfulness, and close inquiry, notwithstanding the attempts to evade and conceal, will generally reveal the true state of the case. Then should the mother faithfully present this subject to them in its true light, showing its degrading, downward tendency. Try to convince them that indulgence in this sin will destroy self-respect and nobleness of character; will ruin health and morals, and its foul stain will blot from the soul true love for God, and the beauty of holiness. The mother should pursue this matter until she has sufficient evidence that the practice is at an end.

The course which most mothers pursue, in training their children in this dangerous age, is injurious to their children. It prepares the way to make their ruin more certain. Some mothers, with their own hands, open the door and virtually invite the devil in, by permitting their daughters to remain in idleness, or what is but little better, spend their time in knitting edging, crocheting, or embroidering, and employ a hired girl to do those things their children should do. They let them visit other young friends, form their own acquaintances, and even go from their parental watchcare some distance from home, where they are allowed to do very much as they please. Satan improves all such opportunities, and takes charge of the minds of these children whom mothers ignorantly expose to his artful snares. Because this course was pursued thirty years ago with comparative safety, it is no evidence that it can be now. The present cannot be judged by the past.

Mothers should take their daughters with them into the kitchen, and give them a thorough education in the cooking department. They should also instruct them in the art of substantial sewing. They should teach them how to cut garments economically, and put them together neatly. Some mothers, rather than to take this trouble, to patiently instruct their inexperienced daughters, prefer to do all themselves. But in so doing, they leave the essential branches of education neglected, and commit a great wrong against their children; for in after life they feel embarrassment, because of their lack of knowledge in these things.

Mothers should educate their daughters in regard to the laws of life. They should understand their own frame, and the relation their eating, drinking, and every-day habits, have to health and a sound constitution, without which the sciences would be of but little benefit.

The help of the daughters will often make so much difference with the mother's work, that kitchen help can be dispensed with, which will prove not only a saving of expense, but a continual benefit to the children, by making room for them to labor, and bringing them into the society, and under the direct influence, of their mother, whose duty it is to patiently instruct the dear ones committed to her care. Also, a door will be closed against much evil, which a hired girl may bring into a family. In a few days she may exert a strong influence over the children of the family, and initiate your daughters into the practice of deception and vice.

Children should be instructed from their early years to be helpful, and to share the burdens of their parents. By thus doing, they can be a great blessing in lightening the cares of the weary mother. While children are engaged in active labor, time will not hang heavily upon their hands, and they will have less opportunity to associate with vain, talkative, unsuitable companions, whose evil communications might blight the whole life of an innocent girl, by corrupting her good manners.

Active employment will give but little time to invite Satan's temptations. They may be often weary, but this will not injure them. Nature will restore their vigor and strength in their sleeping hours, if her laws are not violated. And the thoroughly-tired person has less inclination for secret indulgence.

Mothers allow themselves to be deceived in regard to their daughters. If they labor, and then appear languid and indisposed, the indulgent mother fears that she has overtaxed them, and resolves henceforward to lighten their task. The mother bears the extra amount of labor which should have been performed by the daughters. If the true facts in the case of many were known, it would be seen that it was not the labor which was the cause of the difficulty, but wrong habits which were prostrating the vital energies, and bringing upon them a sense of weakness and great debility. In such cases, when mothers relieve their daughters from active labor, they, by so doing, virtually give them up to idleness, to reserve their energies. to consume upon the altar of lust. They remove the obstacles, giving the mind more freedom to run in a wrong channel, where they will more surely carry on the work of self-ruin.

The state of our world is alarming. Everywhere we look, we see imbecility, dwarfed forms, crippled limbs, misshapen heads, and deformity of every description. Sin and crime, and the violation of nature's laws, are the causes of this accumulation of human woe and suffering. A large share of the youth now living are worthless. Corrupt habits are wasting their energies, and bringing upon them loathsome and complicated diseases. Unsuspecting parents will try the skill of physicians, one after another, who prescribe drugs, when they generally know the real cause of the failing health; but for fear of offending, and losing their fees, they keep silent, when, as faithful physicians, they should expose the real cause. Their drugs only add a second great burden for abused nature to struggle against; and in this struggle nature often breaks down in her efforts, and the victim dies. And the friends look upon the death as a mysterious dispensation of Providence, when the most mysterious part of the matter is, that nature bore up as long as she did against her violated laws. Health, reason, and life, were sacrificed to depraved lusts.

Children who practice self-indulgence previous to puberty, or the period of merging into manhood or womanhood, must pay the penalty of nature's violated laws at that critical period. Many sink into an early grave, while others have sufficient force of constitution to pass this ordeal. If the practice is continued from the age of fifteen and upward, nature will protest against the abuse she has suffered, and continues to suffer, and will make them pay the penalty for the transgression of her laws, especially from the ages of thirty to forty-five, by numerous pains in the system, and various diseases, such as affection of the liver and lungs, neuralgia, rheumatism, affection of the spine, diseased kidneys, and cancerous humors. Some of nature's fine machinery gives way, leaving a heavier task for the remaining to perform, which disorders nature's fine arrangement, and there is often a sudden breaking down of the constitution; and death is the result.

Mothers, you should give your children enough to do. If they get weary, it will not injure health. There is quite a difference between weariness and exhaustion. Indolence will not be favorable to physical, mental, or moral, health. It throws open the door, and invites Satan in, which opportunity he improves, and draws the young into his snares. By indolence, not only the moral strength is weakened, and the impulse of passion increased, but Satan's angels take possession of the whole citadel of the mind, and compel conscience to surrender to vile passion. We should teach our children habits of patient industry. We should beware of indulging them too much. When they meet with difficulty in their labor, we must help them through it instead of carrying them over it. It might be easier for us at the time to do the latter; but we fail to teach a useful and valuable lesson of self-reliance to our children, and are preparing the way to greatly increase our cares in the end. We should awaken in our children generous, noble principles, and urge them to active exertions, which will shield them from a multitude of temptations, and make their lives happier.

My sisters, as mothers we are responsible in a great degree for the physical, mental, and moral, health of our children. We can do much by teaching them correct habits of living. We can show them, by our example, that we make a great account of health, and that they should not violate its laws. We should not make it a practice to place upon our tables food which would injure the health of our children. Our food should be prepared free from spices. Mince pies, cakes, preserves, and highly-seasoned meats, with gravies, create a feverish condition in the system, and inflame the animal passions. We should teach our children to practice habits of self-denial; that the great battle of life is with self, to restrain the passions, and bring them into subjection to the mental and moral faculties.

My sisters, be entreated to spend less time over the cook-stove, preparing food to tempt the appetite, and thus wearing out the strength given you of God to be used for a better purpose. A plain, nourishing diet will not require so great an amount of labor. We should devote more time to humble, earnest prayer to God, for wisdom to bring up our children in the nurture and admonition of the Lord. The health of the mind is dependent upon the health of the body. As Christian parents, we are bound to train our children in reference to the laws of life. We should instruct them, by precept and example, that we do not live to eat, but that we eat to live. We should encourage in our children a love for nobleness of mind, and a pure, virtuous character. In order to strengthen in them the moral perceptions, the love of spiritual things, we must regulate the manner of our living, dispense with animal food, and use grains, vegetables, and fruits, as articles of diet.

Mothers, is there not a work for you to do in your families? You may inquire, How can we remedy the evils which already exist? How shall we begin the work? If you lack wisdom, go to God. He has promised to give liberally. Pray much, and fervently, for divine aid. One rule cannot be followed in every case. The exercise of sanctified judgment is now needful. Be not hasty and agitated, and approach your children with censure. Such a course would only cause rebellion in them. You should feel deeply over any wrong course you have taken, which may have opened a door for Satan to lead your children by his temptations. If you have not instructed them in regard to the violation of the laws of health, blame rests upon you. You have neglected an important duty, the result of which may be seen in the wrong practices of your children. Before you engage in the work of teaching your children the lesson of self-control, you should learn it yourself. If you are easily agitated, and become impatient, how can you appear reasonable to your children while instructing them to control their passions? With self-possession, and feelings of the deepest sympathy and pity, you should approach your erring children, and faithfully present to them the sure work of ruin upon their constitutions, if they continue the course they have begun; that as they debilitate the physical and mental, so, also, the moral must feel the decay, and they are sinning, not only against themselves, but against God.

You should make them feel, if possible, that it is God, the pure and holy God, that they have been sinning against; that the great Searcher of hearts is displeased with their course; that nothing is concealed from him. If you can so impress your children, that they will exercise that repentance which is acceptable to God, that godly sorrow which worketh repentance unto salvation, not to be repented of, the work will be thorough, the reform certain. They will not feel sorrow merely because their sins are known; but they will view their sinful practices in their aggravated character, and will be led to confess them to God, without reserve, and will forsake them. They will feel to sorrow for their wrong course, because they have displeased God, and sinned against him, and dishonored their bodies before Him who created them, and has required them to present their bodies a living sacrifice, holy and acceptable unto him, which is their reasonable service.

"What! know ye not that your body is the temple of the Holy Ghost which is in you, which ye have of God, and ye are not your own? For ye are bought with a price; therefore glorify God in your body, and in your spirit, which are God's." 1 Corinthians 6:19, 20.

You should present encouragements before your children that a merciful God will accept true heart repentance, and will bless their endeavors to cleanse themselves from all filthiness of the flesh and spirit. As Satan sees that he is losing control over the minds of your children, he will strongly tempt them and seek to bind them to continue to practice this bewitching vice. But with a firm purpose they must resist Satan's temptations to indulge the animal passions, because it is sin against God. They should not venture on forbidden ground, where Satan can claim control over them. If they in humility entreat God for purity of thought, and a refined and sanctified imagination, he will hear them, and grant their petitions. God has not left them to perish in their sins, but will help the weak and helpless, if they cast themselves in faith upon him. Those who have been in the practice of secret indulgence until they have prostrated their physical and mental strength, may never fully recover from the result of the violation of nature's laws; but their only salvation in this world, and that which is to come, depends upon entire reform. Every deviation is making recovery more hopeless. None should be discouraged if they perceive no decided improvement in their health after the habit has been broken off for quite a length of time. If nature's laws have not been too long abused, she will carry on her restoring process, although it may not be immediately realized. But some have so long abused nature that she cannot recover entirely. Such must reap as long as they live, to a greater or less degree, the fruit of their doings.

We do not charge all the youth who are feeble of being guilty of wrong habits. There are those who are pure-minded and conscientious, who are sufferers from different causes over which they have no control.

The only sure safety for our children against every vicious practice is, to seek to be admitted into the fold of Christ, and to be taken under the watchcare of the faithful and true Shepherd. He will save them from every evil, shield them from all dangers, if they will heed his voice. He says, "My sheep hear my voice, and they follow me." In Christ they will find pasture, obtain strength and hope, and will not be troubled with restless longings for something to divert the mind, and satisfy the heart. They have found the pearl of great price, and the mind is at peaceful rest. Their pleasures are of a pure, elevated, heavenly character. They leave no painful reflections, no remorse. Such pleasures do not enfeeble the body, nor prostrate the mind, but give health and vigor to both.

Communion with, and love for, God, the practice of holiness, the destruction of sin, are all pleasant. The reading of God's word does not fascinate the imagination, and inflame the passions, like a fictitious story book, but softens, soothes, elevates, and sanctifies, the heart. When the youth are in trouble, when assailed by fierce temptations, they have the privilege of prayer. What an exalted privilege! Finite beings, of dust and ashes, admitted, through the mediation of Christ, into the audience-chamber of the Most High. In such exercises the soul is brought into a sacred nearness with God, and is renewed in knowledge, and true holiness, and fortified against the assaults of the enemy.

No matter how high a person's profession, those who are willing to be employed in gratifying the lust of the flesh, cannot be Christians. As servants of Christ, their employment, and meditations, and pleasure, should consist in things more excellent.

Many are ignorant of the sinfulness of these habits, and their certain results. Such need to be enlightened. Some who profess to be followers of Christ, know that they are sinning against God and ruining their health, yet they are slaves to their own corrupt passions. They feel a guilty conscience, and have less and less inclination to approach God in secret prayer. They may keep up the form of religion, yet be destitute of the grace of God in the heart. They have no devotedness to his service, no trust in him, no living to his glory, no pleasure in his ordinances, and no delight in him. The first commandment requires every living being to love and serve God with all the might, mind, and strength. Especially should professed Christians understand the principles of acceptable obedience.

Can any expect that God will accept a profession, a form, merely, while the heart is withheld, and they refuse to obey his commandments? They sacrifice physical strength and reason upon the altar of lust, and can they think that God will accept their distracted, imbecile service, while they continue their wrong course? Such are just as surely self-murderers as though they pointed a pistol to their own breast, and destroyed their life instantly. In the first case they linger longer, are more debilitated, and destroy gradually the vital force of their constitution, and the mental faculties; yet the work of decay is sure. While they live, they curse the earth with their imbecile influence, are a stumbling-block to sinners, and cause their friends living sorrow, and an immeasurable weight of anxiety and care as they mark the signs of their decay, and have daily evidence of their impaired intellect.

To take one's life instantly is no greater sin in the sight of Heaven than to destroy it gradually, but surely. Persons who bring upon themselves sure decay by wrong-doing, will suffer the penalty here, and, without a thorough repentance, will not be admitted into Heaven hereafter, any sooner than the one who destroys life instantly. The will of God establishes the connection between cause and its effects. Fearful consequences are attached to the least violation of God's law. All will seek to avoid the result, but will not labor to avoid the cause which produced the result. The cause is wrong, the effect right, the knowledge of which is to restrain the transgressor.

The inhabitants of Heaven are perfect, because the will of God is their joy and supreme delight. Many here destroy their own comfort, injure their health, and violate a good conscience, because they will not cease to do wrong. The injunction to mortify the deeds of the body, with its affections and lusts, has no effect upon them. They profess Christ, but are not his followers, and never can be until they cease their wrong-doing, and work the work of righteousness.

Females possess less vital force than the other sex, and are deprived very much of the bracing, invigorating air, by their indoor life. The result of self-abuse in them is seen in various diseases, such as catarrh, dropsy, headache, loss of memory and sight, great weakness in the back and loins, affections of the spine, and frequently, inward decay of the head. Cancerous humor, which would lie dormant in the system their lifetime, is inflamed, and commences its eating, destructive work. The mind is often utterly ruined, and insanity supervenes.

The only hope for those who practice vile habits is to leave them forever, if they place any value upon health here, and salvation hereafter. When these habits have been indulged in for quite a length of time, it requires a determined effort to resist temptation, and refuse the corrupt indulgence. Those who destroy themselves by their own acts will never have eternal life. They that will continue to abuse the health and life given them of God in this world, would not make a right use of health and immortal life were they granted them in God's everlasting kingdom.

The practice of secret habits surely destroys the vital forces of the system. All unnecessary vital action will be followed by corresponding depression. Among the young, the vital capital, and the brain, are so severely taxed at an early age, that there is a deficiency and great exhaustion, which leave the system exposed to diseases of various kinds. But the most common of these is consumption. None can live when their vital energies are used up. They must die. God hates everything impure, and his frown is upon all who give themselves up to gradual and sure decay.

"Know ye not that ye are the temple of God, and that the Spirit of God dwelleth in you? If any man defile the temple of

God, him shall God destroy; for the temple of God is holy, which temple ye are. 1 Corinthians 3:16, 17.

Those who corrupt their own bodies cannot enjoy the favor of God, until they sincerely repent, make an entire reform, and perfect holiness in the fear of the Lord. None can be Christians and indulge in habits which debilitate the system, bring on a state of prostration of the vital forces, and end in making a complete wreck of beings formed in the image of God. This moral pollution will certainly bring its reward. The cause must produce the results. Those who profess to be disciples of Christ should be elevated in all their thoughts and acts, and should ever realize that they are fitting for immortality, and that, if saved, they must be without spot, or wrinkle, or any such thing. Their Christian character must be without a blemish, or they will be pronounced unfit to be taken to a holy Heaven, to dwell with pure, sinless beings in God's everlasting kingdom.

It is the special work of Satan in these last days to take possession of the minds of youth, to corrupt their thoughts, and inflame their passions, knowing that by thus doing he can lead them to self-pollution, and then all the noble faculties of the mind will become debased, and he can control them to suit his own purposes. All are free moral agents; and as such they must bring their thoughts to run in the right channel. Their meditations should be of that nature which will elevate their minds, and make Jesus and Heaven the subjects of their thoughts. Here is a wide field in which the mind can safely range. If Satan seeks to divert the mind from this to low and sensual things, bring it back again, and place it on eternal things; and when the Lord sees the determined effort made to retain only pure thoughts, he will attract the mind, like the magnet, and purify the thoughts, and enable them to cleanse themselves from every secret sin. "Casting down imaginations, and every high thing that exalteth itself against the knowledge of God, and bringing into captivity every thought to the obedience of Christ." 2 Corinthians 10:5. The first work of those who would reform is, to purify the imagination. If the mind is led out in a vicious direction, it must be restrained to dwell only upon pure and elevated subjects. When tempted to yield to a corrupt imagination, then flee to the throne of grace, and pray for strength from Heaven. In the strength of God the imagination can be disciplined to dwell upon things which are pure and heavenly.

Some young persons who have been initiated into the vile practices of the world, seek to awaken the curiosity of other inquisitive minds, and impart to them that secret knowledge, ignorance of which would be bliss. They are not content with practicing themselves the vice they have learned. They are hurried on by the devil, to whisper their evil communications to other minds, to corrupt their good manners. And unless the youth have fixed religious principles, they will be corrupted. A heavy penalty will rest upon those who suffered Satan to use them as mediums to lead astray, and corrupt the minds of others. A heavy curse rested upon the serpent in Eden, because he was the medium Satan used to tempt our first parents to transgress; and a heavy curse from God will follow those who yield themselves as instruments in the subversion of others. And although those who permit themselves to be led astray, and learn vile habits, will suffer for their sin, yet those guilty of instructing them will also suffer for their own sins, and the sins they led others to commit. It were better for such if they had never been born.

Those who would have that wisdom which is from God, must become fools in the sinful knowledge of this age, in order to be wise. They should shut their eyes, that they may see and learn no evil. They should close their ears, lest they hear that which is evil, and obtain that knowledge which would stain their purity of thoughts and acts. And they should guard their tongues, lest they utter corrupt communications, and guile be found in their mouths.

All are accountable for their actions while upon probation in this world. All have power to control their actions. If they are weak in virtue and purity of thoughts and acts, they can obtain help from the Friend of the helpless. Jesus is acquainted with all the weaknesses of human nature, and, if entreated, will give strength to overcome the most powerful temptations. All can obtain this strength if they seek for it in humility. Jesus gives all a blessed invitation who are burdened, and laden with sin, to come to him, the sinner's friend. "Come unto me, all ye that labor, and are heavy laden, and I will give you rest. Take my yoke upon you, and learn of me; for I am meek and lowly in heart; and ye shall find rest to your souls. For my yoke is easy, and my burden is light." Matthew 11:28-30.

Here the most inquisitive may safely learn in the school

of Christ that which will prove for their present and everlasting good. The uneasy and dissatisfied will here find rest. With their thoughts and affections centered in Christ, they will obtain true wisdom, which will be worth more to them than the richest earthly treasures.

Many professed Christians do not labor perseveringly. They make too little effort, and are not ready and willing to deny self. The prayer of the living Christian will be to "be filled with the knowledge of His will, in all wisdom and spiritual understanding, that ye may walk worthy of the Lord unto all pleasing, being fruitful in every good work, and increasing in the knowledge of God, strengthened with all might, according to his glorious power, unto all patience and long-suffering with joyfulness." Colossians 1:9-11. "In whom are hid all the treasures of wisdom and knowledge." Colossians 2:3.

Here is the true knowledge, which should be desired and possessed by every Christian. This knowledge will not lead to ungodliness. It will not break down the constitution, nor bring a gloomy cloud over the mind; but will impart substantial joys and true happiness. This wisdom is divine, and flows ceaselessly from a pure fountain which gives peace, joy, and health.

Even many professed Christians seem to have no earnest desire for this heavenly knowledge, and remain in willing ignorance of this divine grace which it is their privilege to obtain. The only safety for the youth is to seek this precious wisdom, which will assuredly destroy all desire for corrupt knowledge. And when they have acquired a relish for the pure, calm, satisfying joys of faith and holiness, every feeling of their being will rise in abhorrence to corrupting pleasures. All can choose life if they will. They can resist sin, take pleasure in the ways of righteousness and true holiness, and be rewarded with eternal life in God's everlasting kingdom.

If they choose to corrupt their ways before the Lord, defile their own bodies and commit self-murder, they can do so; but they should remember that the judgment is to sit, and the books are to be opened, and they are to be judged out of those things which are written in the books, according to their works. What a fearful, spotted record will be opened before them, of their secret thoughts, and vile acts. Sentence is pronounced upon them, and they are shut out from the city of God, with the ungodly, and miserably perish with the wicked.

Now is the time of preparation. None need to expect that God will do the work of preparing and fitting them up, without their efforts. It is for them to work the works of righteousness, and crowd all the right-doing they can into the little space of time allotted to them before probation closes, that they may have a clean record in Heaven. I close with the entreaty of the prophet, "Turn ye, turn ye, from your evil ways; for why will ye die?" Ezekiel 33:11.

Chapter 2

The Marriage Relation

Men and women, by indulging the appetite with rich and highly-seasoned foods, especially flesh-meats and rich gravies, and by using stimulating drinks, as tea and coffee, create unnatural appetites. The system becomes fevered, the organs of digestion become injured, the mental faculties are beclouded, while the baser passions are excited, and predominate. The appetite becomes more unnatural, and more difficult of restraint. The circulation is not equalized, and the blood becomes impure. The whole system is deranged, and the demands of appetite become more unreasonable, craving exciting, hurtful things, until it is thoroughly depraved.

With many, the appetite clamors for the disgusting weed, tobacco, and ale, made powerful by poisonous, health-destroying mixtures. Many do not stop even here. Their debased appetites call for stronger drink, which has a still more benumbing influence upon the brain. Thus they give themselves up to every excess, until appetite holds complete control over the reasoning faculties; and man, formed in the image of his Maker, debases himself lower than the beasts. Manhood and honor are alike sacrificed to appetite. It required time to benumb the sensibilities of the mind. It was done gradually, but surely. The indulgence of the appetite in first eating food highly seasoned, created a morbid appetite, and prepared the way for every kind of indulgence, until health and intellect were sacrificed to lust.

Many have entered the marriage relation who have not acquired property, and who have had no inheritance. They did not possess physical strength or mental energy, to acquire property. It has been just such ones who have been in haste to marry, and who have taken upon themselves responsibilities of which they had no just sense. They did not possess noble, elevated feelings, and had no just idea of the duty of a husband and father, and what it would cost them to provide for the wants of a family. And they manifested no more propriety in the increase of their families than that shown in their business transactions. Those who are seriously deficient in business tact, and who are the least qualified to get along in the world, generally fill their houses with children; while men who have ability to acquire property, generally have no more children than they can well provide for. Those who are not qualified to take care of themselves, should not have children. It has been the case that the numerous offspring of these poor calculators are left to come up like the brutes. They are not suitably fed or clothed, and do not receive physical or mental training, and there is nothing sacred in the word home, to either parents or children.

The marriage institution was designed of Heaven to be a blessing to man; but, in a general sense, it has been abused in such a manner as to make it a dreadful curse. Most of men and women have acted, in entering the marriage relation, as though the only question for them to settle was, whether they loved each other. But they should realize that a responsibility rests upon them in the marriage relation farther than this. They should consider whether their offspring will possess physical health, and mental and moral strength. But few have moved with high motives, and with elevated considerations which they could not lightly throw off—that society had claims upon them, that the weight of their family's influence would tell in the upward or downward scale.

Society is composed of families; and heads of families are responsible for the molding of society. If those who choose to enter the marriage relation without due consideration were alone to be the sufferers, then the evil would not be so great, and their sin would be comparatively small. But the misery arising from unhappy marriages is felt by the offspring of such unions. They have entailed upon them a life of living misery; and, though innocent, suffer the consequences of their parents' inconsiderate course. Men and women have no right to follow impulse, or blind passion, in their marriage relation, and then bring innocent children into the world to realize from various causes that life has but little joy, but little happiness, and is therefore a burden. Children generally inherit the peculiar traits of character which the parents possess; and in addition to all this, many

29

come up without any redeeming influence around them. They are too frequently huddled together in poverty and filth. With such surroundings and examples, what can be expected of the children when they come upon the stage of action, but that they will sink lower in the scale of moral worth than their parents, and their deficiencies, in every respect, be more apparent than theirs? Thus have this class perpetuated their deficiencies, and cursed their posterity with poverty, imbecility, and degradation. These should not have married. At least, they should not have brought innocent children into existence to share their misery, and hand down their own deficiencies, with accumulating wretchedness, from generation to generation. This is one great cause of the degeneracy of the race.

If women of past generations had always moved from high considerations, realizing that future generations would be ennobled or debased by their course of action, they would have taken their stand, that they could not unite their life interest with men who were cherishing unnatural appetites for alcoholic drinks, and tobacco which is a slow, but sure and deadly, poison, weakening the nervous system, and debasing the noble faculties of the mind. If men would remain wedded to these vile habits, women should have left them to their life of single blessedness, to enjoy these companions of their choice. Women should not have considered themselves of so little value as to unite their destiny with men who had no control over their appetites, but whose principal happiness consisted in eating and drinking, and gratifying their animal passions. Women have not always followed the dictates of reason. They have sometimes been led by blind impulse. They have not always felt in a high degree the responsibilities resting upon them, to form such life connections as would not enstamp upon their offspring a low degree of morals, and a passion to gratify debased appetites, at the expense of health, and even life. God will hold them accountable in a large degree for the physical health and moral characters thus transmitted to future generations.

Men and women who have corrupted their own bodies by dissolute habits, have also debased their intellects and destroyed the fine sensibilities of the soul. Very many of this class have married, and left for an inheritance to their offspring the taints of their own physical debility and depraved morals. The gratification of animal passions and gross sensuality have been the marked characteristics of their posterity, which have descended from generation to generation, increasing human misery to a fearful degree, and hastening the deterioration of the race.

Men and women who have become sickly and diseased, have often in their marriage connections selfishly thought only of their own happiness. They have not seriously considered the matter from the standpoint of noble, elevated principles, reasoning in regard to what they could expect of their posterity, but diminished energy of body and mind which would not elevate society, but sink it still lower.

Sickly men have often won the affections of women apparently healthy, and because they loved each other, they have felt themselves at perfect liberty to marry, neither considering that

31

by their union the wife must be a sufferer, more or less, because of the diseased husband. In many cases, the diseased husband improves in health, while the wife shares his disease. He lives very much upon her vitality, and she soon complains of failing health. He prolongs his days by shortening the days of his wife. Those who thus marry, commit sin in lightly regarding health and life given to them of God to be used to his glory. But if those who thus enter the marriage relation were alone concerned, the sin would not be so great. Their offspring are compelled to be sufferers by disease transmitted to them. Thus disease has been perpetuated from generation to generation. And many charge all this weight of human misery upon God, when their wrong course of action has brought the sure result. They have thrown upon society an enfeebled race, and done their part to deteriorate the race, by rendering disease hereditary, and thus accumulating human suffering.

Another cause of the deficiency of the present generation in physical strength and moral worth, is the union of men and women in marriage whose ages widely differ. It is frequently the case that old men choose to marry young wives. By thus doing the life of the husband has often been prolonged, while the wife has had to feel the want of that vitality which she has imparted to her aged husband. It has not been the duty of any woman to sacrifice life and health, even if she did love one so much older than herself, and felt willing on her part to make such a sacrifice. She should have restrained her affections. She had considerations higher than her own interest to consult. She should consider, if children were born to them, what their condition would be. It is still worse for young men to marry women considerably older than themselves. The offspring of such unions in many cases, where ages widely differ, have not well-balanced minds. They have been deficient also in physical strength. In such families, varied, peculiar, and often painful, traits of character have frequently been manifested. The children often die pre-maturely, and those who reach maturity, in many cases, are deficient in physical and mental strength, and moral worth.

The father is seldom prepared, with his failing faculties, to properly bring up his young family. These children have peculiar traits of character, which constantly need a counteracting influence, or they will go to certain ruin. They are not educated aright. Their discipline has too often been of the fitful, impulsive kind, by reason of his age. The father has been susceptible of changeable feelings. At one time over-indulgent, while at another he is unwarrantably severe. Everything in such families is wrong, and domestic wretchedness is greatly increased. Thus a class of beings have been thrown upon the world as a burden to society.

Those who increase their number of children, when, if they consulted reason, they must know that physical and mental weakness must be their inheritance, are transgressors of the last six precepts of God's law, which specify the duty of man to his fellow-man. They do their part in increasing the degeneracy of the race, and in sinking society lower, thus injuring their neighbor. If God thus regards the rights of neighbors, has he no care in regard to closer and more sacred relationship? If not a sparrow falls to the ground without his notice, will he be unmindful of the children born into the world, diseased physically and mentally, suffering in a greater or less degree, all their lives? Will he not call parents to an account, to whom he has given reasoning powers, for putting these higher faculties in the background, and becoming slaves to passion, when, as the result, generations must bear the mark of their physical, mental, and moral deficiencies? In addition to the suffering they entail upon their children, they have no portion but poverty to leave to their pitiful flock. They cannot educate them, and many do not see the necessity of it; neither could they, if they did see such necessity, find time to train them, and instruct them, and lessen, as much as possible, the wretched inheritance transmitted to them. Parents should not increase their families any faster than they know that their children can be well cared for, and educated. A child in the mother's arms from year to year is great injustice to her. It lessens, and often destroys, social enjoyment, and increases domestic wretchedness. It robs their children of that care, education, and happiness, which parents should feel it their duty to bestow upon them.

The husband violates the marriage vow and the duties enjoined upon him in the word of God, when he disregards the health and happiness of the wife, by increasing her burdens and cares by numerous offspring. "Husbands, love your wives, even as Christ also loved the church, and gave himself for it. So ought men to love their wives as their own bodies. He that loveth his wife loveth himself. For no man ever yet hated his own flesh, but nourisheth and cherisheth it, even as the Lord the church."

We see this holy injunction almost wholly disregarded, even by professed Christians. Everywhere you may look, you will see pale, sickly, careworn, broken-down, dispirited, discouraged women. They are generally overworked, and their vital energies exhausted by frequent child-bearing. The world is filled with images of human beings who are of no worth to society. Many are deficient in intellect, and many who possess natural talents do not use them for any beneficial purposes. They are not cultivated, and the one great reason is, children have been multiplied faster than they could be well trained, and have been left to come up much like the brutes.

The Care of Children

Children in this age are suffering with their parents, more or less, the penalty of the violation of the laws of health. The course generally pursued with them, from their infancy, is in continual opposition to the laws of their being. They were compelled to receive a miserable inheritance of disease and debility, before their birth, occasioned by the wrong habits of their parents, which will affect them in a greater or less degree through life. This bad state of things is made every way worse by parents' continuing to follow a wrong course in the physical training of their children during their childhood.

Parents manifest astonishing ignorance, indifference, and recklessness, in regard to the physical health of their children, which often results in destroying the little vitality left the abused infant, and consigns it to an early grave. You will frequently hear parents mourning over the providence of God which has torn their children from their embrace. Our Heavenly Father is too wise to err, and too good to do us wrong. He has no delight in seeing his creatures suffer. Thousands have been ruined for life because parents have not acted in accordance with the laws of health. They have moved from impulse, instead of following the dictates of sound judgment, constantly having in view the future well being of their children.

The first great object to be attained in the training of children is soundness of constitution, which will prepare the way, in a great measure for mental and moral training. Physical and moral health are closely united. What an enormous weight of responsibility is seen to rest upon parents, when we consider that the course pursued by them, before the birth of their children, has very much to do with the development of their characters after their birth.

Many children are left to come up with less attention from their parents than a good farmer devotes to his dumb animals. Fathers, especially, are often guilty of manifesting less care for wife and children than that shown to their cattle. A merciful farmer will take time, and devote especial thought as to the best manner of managing his stock, and will be particular that his valuable horses shall not be overworked, overfed, or fed when heated, lest they be ruined. He will take time and care for his stock, lest they be injured by neglect, exposure, or any improper treatment, and his increasing young stock depreciate in value. He will observe regular periods for their eating, and will know the amount of work they can perform without injuring them. In order to accomplish this, he will provide them only the most healthful food, in proper quantities, and at stated periods. By thus following the dictates of reason, farmers are successful in preserving the strength of their beasts. If the interest of every father, for his wife and children, corresponded to that care manifested for his cattle, in that degree that their lives are more valuable than the dumb animals, there would be an entire reformation in every family, and human misery be far less.

Great care should be manifested by parents in providing them the most healthful articles of food for themselves and for their children. And in no case should they place before their children food which their reason teaches them is not conducive to health, but which would fever the system, and derange the digestive organs. Parents do not study from cause to effect in regard to their children, as in the case of their dumb animals, and do not reason that to overwork, to eat after violent exercise, and when much exhausted, and heated, will injure the health of human beings, as well as the health of dumb animals, and will lay the foundation for a broken constitution in man, as well as in beasts.

The father in many cases exercises more reason respecting, and manifests more care for, his cattle when with young, than he manifests for his wife, when in a similar condition. The mother, in many cases previous to the birth of her children, is permitted to toil early and late, heating her blood, while preparing various unhealthful dishes of food to suit the perverted taste of the family, and of visitors. Her strength should be tenderly cherished. A preparation of healthful food would require but about one-half of the expense and labor, and would be far more nourishing.

The mother, before the birth of her children, is often permitted to labor beyond her strength. Her burdens and cares are seldom lessened, and that period, which should be to her of all others, a time of rest, is one of fatigue, sadness, and gloom. By too great exertion on her part, she deprives her offspring of that nutrition which nature has provided for it, and by heating her blood, she imparts to it a bad quality of nourishment. The offspring is robbed of its vitality, robbed of physical and mental strength. The father should study how to make the mother happy. He should not allow himself to come to his home with a clouded brow. It he is perplexed in business, he should not, unless it is actually necessary to counsel with his wife, trouble her with such matters. She has cares and trials of her own to bear, and she should be tenderly spared every needless burden.

The mother too often meets with cold reserve from the father. If everything does not move off just as pleasantly as he could wish, he blames the wife and mother, and seems indifferent to her cares and daily trials. Men who do this are working directly against their own interest and happiness. The mother becomes discouraged. Hope and cheerfulness depart from her. She goes about her work mechanically, knowing that it must be done, which soon debilitates physical and mental health. Children are born to them, suffering from various diseases, and God holds the parents accountable in a great degree; for it was their wrong habits which fastened disease upon their unborn children, under which they are compelled to suffer all through their lives. Some live but a short period with their load of debility. The mother anxiously watches over the life of her child, and is weighed down with sorrow as she is compelled to close its eyes in death, and she often regards God as the author of all this affliction, when the parents in reality were the murderers of their own child.

The father should bear in mind that the treatment of his wife before the birth of his offspring will materially affect the disposition of the mother during that period, and will have very much to do with the character developed by the child after its birth. Many fathers have been so anxious to obtain property fast, that higher considerations have been sacrificed and some men have been criminally neglectful of the mother and her offspring, and too frequently the lives of both have been sacrificed to the strong desire to accumulate wealth. Many do not immediately suffer this heavy penalty for their wrong-doing, and are asleep to the result of their course. The condition of the wife is sometimes no better that than of a slave, and sometimes she is equally guilty with the husband, of squandering physical strength, to obtain means to live fashionably. It is a crime for such to have children, for their offspring will often be deficient in physical, mental, and moral worth, and will bear the miserable, close, selfish impress of their parents; and the world will be cursed with their meanness.

It is the duty of men and women to act with reason in regard to their labor. They should not exhaust their energies unnecessarily, for by doing this, they not only bring suffering upon themselves, but, by their errors, bring anxiety, weariness, and suffering, upon those they love. What calls for such an amount of labor? Intemperance in eating and in drinking, and the desire for wealth, have led to this intemperance in labor. If the appetite is controlled, and that food only which is healthful be taken, there will be so great a saving of expense, that men and women will not be compelled to labor beyond their strength, and thus violate the laws of health. The desire of men and women to accumulate property is not sinful, if, in their efforts to attain their object, they do not forget God, and transgress the last six precepts of Jehovah, which dictate the duty of man to his fellow-man, and place themselves in a position where it is impossible for them to glorify God in their bodies and spirits which are his. If, in their haste to be rich, they overtax their energies and violate the laws of their being, they place themselves in a condition where they cannot render to God perfect service, and are pursuing a course of sin. Property thus obtained is at an immense sacrifice.

Hard labor and anxious care often make the father nervous, impatient, and exacting. He does not notice the tired look of his wife, who has labored, with her feebler strength, just as hard as he has labored, with his stronger energies. He suffers himself to be hurried with business, and, through his anxiety to be rich, loses in a great measure the sense of his obligation to his family, and does not measure aright his wife's power of endurance.

He often enlarges his farm, requiring an increase of hired help, which necessarily increases the housework. The wife realizes every day that she is doing too much work for her strength, yet she toils on, thinkIng the work must be done. She is continually reaching down into the future, drawing upon her future resources of strength, and is living upon borrowed capital, and at the period when she needs that strength, it is not at her command; and if she does not lose her life, her constitution is broken, past recovery.

If the father would become acquainted with physical law, he might better understand his obligations and his responsibilities. He would see that he had been guilty of almost murdering his children, by suffering so many burdens to come upon the mother, compelling her to labor beyond her strength before their birth, in order to obtain means to leave for them. They nurse these children through their suffering life, and often lay them prematurely in the grave, little realizing that their wrong course has brought the sure result. How much better to have shielded the mother of his children from wearing labor and mental anxiety, and let the children inherit good constitutions, and give them an opportunity to battle their way through life, not relying upon their father's property, but upon their own energetic strength. The experience thus obtained would be of more worth to them than houses and lands, purchased at the expense of the health of mother and children.

It seems perfectly natural for some men to be morose, selfish, exacting, and overbearing. They have never learned the lesson of self-control, and will not restrain their unreasonable feelings, let the consequences be what they may. Such men will be repaid, by seeing their companions sickly and dispirited, and their children bearing the peculiarities of their own disagreeable traits of character.

It is the duty of every married couple to studiously avoid marring the feelings of each other. They should control every look and expression of fretfulness and passion. They should study each other's happiness, in small matters, as well as in large, manifesting a tender thoughtfulness, in acknowledging kind acts and the little courtesies of each other. These small things should not be neglected, for they are just as important to the happiness of man and wife, as food is necessary to sustain physical strength. The father should encourage wife and mother to lean upon his large affections. Kind, cheerful, encouraging words from him with whom she has intrusted her life happiness, will be more beneficial to her than any medicine; and the cheerful rays of light which such sympathizing words will bring to the heart of the wife and mother, will reflect back their own cheering beams upon the heart of the father.

The husband will frequently see his wife care-worn and debilitated, growing prematurely old, in laboring to prepare food to suit the vitiated taste. He gratifies the appetite, and will eat and drink those things which it costs much time and labor to prepare for the table, and which have a tendency to make those who partake of them nervous and irritable. The wife and mother is seldom free from the headache, and the children are suffering the effects of eating unwholesome food, and there is a great lack of patience and affection with parents and children. All are sufferers together, for health has been sacrificed to lustful appetite. The offspring, before its birth, has had transmitted to it disease and an unhealthy appetite. And the irritability, nervousness, and despondency, manifested by the mother, will mark the character of her child.

In past generations, if mothers had informed themselves in regard to the laws of their being, they would have understood that their constitutional strength, as well as the tone of their morals, and their mental faculties, would in a great measure be represented in their offspring. Their ignorance upon this subject, where so much is involved, is criminal. Many women never should have become mothers. Their blood was filled with scrofula, transmitted to them from their parents, and increased by their gross manner of living. The intellect has been brought down and enslaved to serve the animal appetites, and children, born of such parents, have been poor sufferers, and of but little use to society.

It has been one of the greatest causes of degeneracy in generations back, up to the present time, that wives and mothers who otherwise would have had a beneficial influence upon society, in raising the standard of morals, have been lost to society through multiplicity of home cares, because of the fashionable, health-destroying manner of cooking, and also in consequence of too frequent child-bearing. She has been compelled to needless suffering, her constitution has failed, and her intellect has become weakened, by so great a draught upon her vital resources. Her offspring suffer her debility, and thus a class is thrown upon society, poorly fitted, through the mother's inability to educate them, to be of the least benefit.

If these mothers had given birth to but few children, and if they had been careful to live upon such food as would preserve physical health and mental strength, so that the moral and intellectual might predominate over the animal, they could have so educated their children for usefulness, as to have made them bright ornaments to society.

If parents in past generations had, with firmness of purpose, kept the body servant to the mind, and had not allowed the intellectual to be enslaved by animal passions, there would be in this age a different order of beings upon the earth. And if the mother, before the birth of her offspring, had always possessed self-control, realizing that she was giving the stamp of character to future generations, the present state of society would not be so depreciated in character as at the present time.

Every woman about to become a mother, whatever may be her surroundings, should encourage constantly a happy, cheerful, contented disposition, knowing that for all her efforts in this direction she will be repaid tenfold in the physical, as well as the moral, character of her offspring. Nor is this all. She can, by habit, accustom herself to cheerful thinking, and thus encourage a happy state of mind, and cast a cheerful reflection of her own happiness of spirit upon her family, and those with whom she associates. And in a very great degree will her physical health be improved. A force will be imparted to the life springs, the blood will not move sluggishly, as would be the case if she were to yield to despondency and gloom. Her mental and moral health are invigorated by the buoyancy of her spirits. The power of the will can resist impressions of the mind, and will prove a grand soother of the nerves. Children who are robbed of that vitality which they should have inherited of their parents, should have the utmost care. By close attention to the laws of their being, a much better condition of things can be established.

The period during which the infant receives its nourishment from the mother, is a critical one. Many mothers, while nursing their infants, have been permitted to overlabor, and to heat their blood in cooking, and the nursling has been seriously affected, not only with fevered nourishment from the mother's breast, but its blood has been poisoned by the unhealthy diet of the mother, which has fevered her whole system, thereby affecting the food of the infant. The infant will also be affected by the condition of the mother's mind. If she is unhappy, easily agitated, irritable, giving vent to outbursts of passion, the nourishment the infant receives from its mother will be inflamed, often producing colic, spasms, and, in some instances, causing convulsions and fits.

The character also of the child is more or less affected by the nature of the nourishment received from the mother. How important, then, that the mother, while nursing her infant, should preserve a happy state of mind, having the perfect control of her own spirit. By thus doing, the food of the child is not injured, and the calm, self-possessed course the mother pursues in the treatment of her child has very much to do in molding the mind of the infant. If it is nervous, and easily agitated, the mother's careful, unhurried manner will have a soothing and correcting influence, and the health of the infant can be very much improved.

Infants have been greatly abused by improper treatment. If fretful, they have generally been fed to keep them quiet, when, in most cases, the very reason of their fretfulness was because of their having received too much food, made injurious by the wrong habits of the mother. More food only made the matter worse, for their stomachs were already overloaded.

Children are generally brought up from the cradle to indulge the appetite, and are taught that they live to eat. The mother does much toward the formation of the character of her children in their childhood. She can teach them to control the appetite, or she can teach them to indulge the appetite, and become gluttons. The mother often arranges her plans to accomplish a certain amount through the day, and when the children trouble her, instead of taking time to soothe their little sorrows, and divert them, something is given them to eat, to keep them still, which answers the purpose for a short time, but eventually makes things worse. The children's stomachs have been pressed with food, when they had not the least want of it. All that was required was a little of the mother's time and attention. But she regarded her time as altogether too precious to devote to the amusement of her children. Perhaps the arrangement of her house in a tasteful manner for visitors to praise, and to have her food cooked in a fashionable style, are with her higher considerations than the happiness and health of her children.

Intemperance in eating and in labor debilitates the parents, often making them nervous, and disqualifying them to rightly discharge their duty to their children. Three times a day, parent and children gather around the table loaded with a variety of fashionable foods. The merits of each dish have to be tested. Perhaps the mother had toiled till she was heated and exhausted, and was not in a condition to take even the simplest food till she had first had a period of rest. The food she wearied herself in preparing was wholly unfit for her at any time, but especially taxes the digestive organs when the blood is heated and the system exhausted. Those who have thus persisted in violating the laws of their being, have been compelled to pay the penalty at some period in their life.

There are ample reasons why there are so many nervous women in the world, complaining of the dyspepsia, with its train of evils. The cause has been followed by the effect. It is impossible for intemperate persons to be patient. They must first reform bad habits, learn to live healthfully, and then it will not be difficult for them to be patient. Many do not seem to understand the relation the mind sustains to the body. If the system is deranged by improper food, the brain and nerves are affected, and slight things annoy those who are thus afflicted. Little difficulties are to them troubles mountain high. Persons thus situated are unfitted to properly train their children. Their life will be marked with extremes. Sometimes they are very indulgent, at other times severe, censuring for trifles which deserve no notice.

The mother frequently sends her children from her presence, because she thinks she cannot endure the noise occasioned by their happy frolics. But with no mother's eye over them to approbate or disapprove at the right time, unhappy differences often arise. A word from the mother would set all right again. They soon become weary, desire change, and go into the street for amusement; and pure, innocent-minded children are driven into bad company, and evil communications breathed into their ears corrupt their good manners. The mother often seems to be asleep to the interests of her children until she is painfully aroused by the exhibition of vice. The seeds of evil were sown in their young minds, promising an abundant harvest. And it is a marvel to her that her children are so prone to do wrong. Parents should begin in season to instill into infant minds good and correct principles. The mother should be with her children as much as possible, and should sow precious seed in their hearts.

The mother's time belongs in a special manner to her children. They have a right to her time which no others can have. In many cases mothers have neglected to discipline their children, because it would require too much of their time, which time they think must be spent in the cooking department, or in preparing their own clothing, and that of their children, according to fashion, to foster pride in their young hearts. In order to keep their restless children still, they have given them cake or candies, at almost any hour of the day, and their stomachs are crowded with hurtful things at irregular periods. Their pale faces testify to the fact that mothers are doing what they can to destroy the remaining life-forces of their poor children. The digestive organs are constantly taxed, and are not allowed periods of rest. The liver becomes inactive, and the blood impure; and the children are sickly and irritable, because they are real sufferers from intemperance, and it is impossible for them to exercise patience.

Parents wonder that children are so much more difficult to control than they used to be. In most cases their own criminal management has made them so. The quality of food they bring upon their tables, and encourage their children to eat, is constantly exciting their animal passions, and weakening the moral and intellectual faculties. Very many children are made miserable dyspeptics in their youth by the wrong course their parents have pursued toward them in childhood. Parents will be called to render an account to God for thus dealing with their children.

Many parents do not give their children lessons in self-control. They indulge their appetite, and suffer them to form, in their childhood, habits of eating and drinking according to their own desires. So will they be in their general habits in their youth. Their desires have not been restrained, and as they grow older, they will not only indulge in the common habits of intemperance, but they will go still further in indulgences. They will choose their own associates, although corrupt. They cannot endure restraint from their parents. They will give loose rein to their corrupt passions, and have but little regard for purity or virtue. This is the reason why there is so little purity and moral worth among the youth of the present day, and is the great cause why men and women feel under so little obligation to render obedience to the law of God. Some parents have not control over themselves. They do not control their own morbid appetites, or their passionate tempers; therefore they cannot educate their children in regard to the denial of their appetite, and teach them self-control.

Errors In Education

Many mothers feel that they have not time to instruct their children, and in order to get them out of the way, and get rid of their noise and trouble, they send them to school. The school-room is a hard place for children who have inherited enfeebled constitutions. School-rooms generally have not been constructed in reference to health, but in regard to cheapness. The rooms have not been arranged so that they could be ventilated as they should have been, without exposing the children to severe colds. And the seats have seldom been made so that the children could sit with ease, and keep their little, growing frames in a proper posture to insure healthy action of the lungs and heart. Young children can grow into almost any shape, and can, by habits of proper exercise and positions of the body, obtain healthy forms. It is destructive to the health and life of young children for them to sit in the school-room, upon hard, ill-formed benches, from three to five hours a day, inhaling the impure air caused by many breaths. The weak lungs become affected, the brain, from which the nervous energy of the whole system is derived, becomes en-feebled by being called into active exercise before the strength of the mental organs is sufficiently matured to endure fatigue.

In the school-room, the foundation has been too surely laid for diseases of various kinds. But, more especially, that most delicate of all organs, the brain, has often been permanently injured by too great exercise. This has often caused inflammation, then dropsy of the head, and convulsions, with their dreaded results. And the lives of many have been thus sacrificed by ambitious mothers. Of those children who have apparently had sufficient force of constitution to survive this treatment, there are very many who carry the effects of it through life. The nervous energy of the brain becomes so weakened, that after they come to maturity, it is impossible for them to endure much mental exercise. The force of some of the delicate organs of the brain seems to be expended.

And not only has the physical and mental health of children been endangered by being sent to school at too early a period, but they have been the losers in a moral point of view. They have had opportunities to become acquainted with children who were uncultivated in their manners, They were thrown into the society of the course and rough, who lie, swear, steal, and deceive, and who delight to impart their knowledge of vice to those younger than themselves. Young children, if left to themselves, learn the bad more readily than the good. Bad habits agree best with the natural heart, and the things which they see and hear in infancy and childhood are deeply imprinted upon their minds, and the bad seed sown in their young hearts will take root, and will become sharp thorns to wound the hearts of their parents.

During the first six or seven years of a child's life, special attention should be given to its physical training, rather than the intellect. After this period, if the physical constitution is good, the education of both should receive attention. Infancy extends to the age of six or seven years. Up to this period, children should be left, like little lambs, to roam around the house and in the yards, skipping and jumping in the buoyancy of their spirits, free from care and trouble.

Parents, especially mothers, should be the only teachers of such infant minds. They should not educate from books. The children will generally be inquisitive to learn the things of nature. They will ask questions in regard to the things they see and hear, and parents should improve the opportunity to instruct, and patiently answer, these little inquirers. They can in this manner get the advantage of the enemy, and fortify the minds of their children, by sowing good seed in their hearts, leaving no room for the bad to take root. The mother's loving instructions is what is needed by children of a tender age in the formation of character.

The first important lesson for children to learn is the proper denial of appetite. It is the duty of mothers to attend to the wants of their children, by soothing and diverting their minds, instead of giving them food, and thus teaching them that eating is the remedy for life's ills.

If parents had lived healthfully, being satisfied with simple diet, much expense would have been saved. The father would not have been obliged to labor beyond his strength, in order to supply the wants of his family. A simple, nourishing diet would not have had an influence to unduly excite the nervous system and the animal passions, producing moroseness and irritability. If he had partaken only of plain food, his head would have been clear, his nerves steady, his stomach in a healthy condition, and with a pure system, he would have had no loss of appetite, and the present generation would be in a much better condition than it now is. But even now, in this late period, something can be done to improve our condition. Temperance in all things is necessary. A temperate father will not complain if he has no great variety upon his table. A healthful manner of living will improve the condition of the family in every sense, and will allow the wife and mother time to devote to her children. The great study with the parents will be in what manner they can best train their children for usefulness in this world, and for Heaven hereafter. They will be content to see their children with neat, plain, but comfortable, garments, free from embroidery and adornment. They will earnestly labor to see their children in the possession of the inward adorning, the ornament of a meek and quiet spirit, which is in the sight of God of great price.

Before the Christian father leaves his home, to go to his labor, he will gather his family around him, and bowing before God will commit them to the care of the Chief Shepherd. He will then go forth to his labor with the love and blessing of his wife, and the love of his children, to make his heart cheerful through his laboring hours. And that mother who is aroused to her duty, will realize the obligations resting upon her to her children in the absence of the father. She will feel that she lives for her husband

and children. By training her children aright, teaching them habits of temperance and self-control, and teaching them their duty to God, she is qualifying them to become useful in the world, to elevate the standard of morals in society, and to reverence and obey the law of God. Patiently and perseveringly will the godly mother instruct her children, giving them line upon line, and precept upon precept, not in a harsh, compelling manner, but in love, and in tenderness; and thus will she win them. They will consider her lessons of love, and will happily listen to her words of instruction.

Instead of sending her children from her presence, that she may not be troubled with their noise, and be annoyed with the numerous attentions they would desire, she will feel that her time cannot be better employed than in soothing, and diverting their restless, active minds with some amusement, or light, happy employment. The mother will be amply repaid for the efforts she may make, and the time she may spend to invent amusement for her children.

Young children love society. They cannot, as a general thing, enjoy themselves alone, and the mother should feel that, in most cases, the place for her children, when they are in the house, is in the room she occupies. She can then have a general oversight of them, and be prepared to set little differences right, when appealed to by them, and correct wrong habits, or the manifestation of selfishness or passion, and can give their minds a turn in the right direction. That which children enjoy, they think mother can be pleased with, and it is perfectly natural for them to consult mother in little matters of perplexity. And the mother should not wound the heart of her sensitive child by treating the matter with indifference, or by refusing to be troubled with such small matters. That which may be small to the mother is large to them. And a word of direction or caution, at the right time, will often prove of great value. An approving glance, a word of encouragement and praise from the mother, will often cast a sunbeam into their young hearts for a whole day.

The first education children should receive from the mother in infancy, should be in regard to their physical health. They should be allowed only plain food, of that quality that will preserve to them the best condition of health, and that should be partaken of only at regular periods, not oftener than three times a day, and two meals would be better than three. If children are disciplined aright, they will soon learn that they can receive nothing by crying or fretting. A judicious mother will act in training her children, not merely in regard to her own present comfort, but for their future good. And to this end, she will teach her children the important lesson of controlling the appetite, and of self-denial, that they should eat, drink, and dress, in reference to health.

A well-disciplined family, who love and obey God, will be cheerful and happy. The father, when he returns from his daily labor, will not bring his perplexities to his home. He will feel that home and the family circle are too sacred to be marred with unhappy perplexities. When he left his home, he did not leave his Saviour and his religion behind. Both were his companions. The sweet influence of his home, the blessing of his wife, and love of his children, make his burdens light, and he returns with peace in his heart, and cheerful, encouraging words for his wife and children, who are waiting to joyfully welcome his coming. As he bows with his family at the altar of prayer, to offer up his grateful thanks to God, for his preserving care of himself and loved ones through the day, angels of God hover in the room, and bear the fervent prayers of God-fearing parents to Heaven, as sweet incense, which are answered by returning blessings.

Parents should impress upon their children that it is sin to consult the taste, to the injury of the stomach. They should impress upon their minds that by violating the laws of their being, they sin against their Maker. Children thus educated will not be difficult of restraint. They will not be subject to irritable, changeable tempers, and will be in a far better condition for enjoying life. Such children will the more readily and clearly understand their moral obligations. Children who have been taught to yield their will and wishes to their parents, will the more easily and readily yield their wills to God, and will submit to be controlled by the Spirit of Christ. Why so many who claim to be Christians have numerous trials, which keep the church burdened, is because they were not correctly trained in their childhood, but were left in a great measure to form their own character. Their wrong habits, and peculiar, unhappy dispositions, were not corrected. They were not taught to yield their will to their parents. Their whole religious experience is affected by their training in childhood. They were not then controlled. They grew up undisciplined, and now, in their religious experience, it is difficult for them to yield to that pure discipline taught in the word of God. Parents should, then, realize the responsibility resting upon them to educate their children in reference to their religious experience.

Those who regard the marriage relation as one of God's sacred ordinances, guarded by his holy precept, will be controlled by the dictates of reason. They will consider carefully the result of every privilege the marriage relation grants. Such will feel that their children are precious jewels committed to their keeping by God, to remove from their natures the rough surface by discipline, that their luster may appear. They will feel under most solemn obligations to so form their characters that they may do good in their life, bless others with their light, and the world be better for their having lived in it, and they be finally fitted for the higher life, the better world, to shine in the presence of God and the Lamb forever.

Chapter 3

Obedience to the Law of God

Mercy and truth are promised to the humble and penitent, and judgments are prepared for the sinful and rebellious. "Justice and judgment are the habitation of Thy throne." Ps. 89:14. A wicked and adulterous people will not escape the wrath of God, the punishment they have justly earned. Man has fallen, and his is a work of a lifetime, beit longer or shorter, to recover from his fall, and regain, throughChrist, the image of the divine, which he has lost by sin and continued transgression. God requires a thorough transformation of soul, body, andspirit, in order to regain the estate lost through Adam. The Lordmercifully sends rays of light to show man his true condition. If he will not walk in the light, he manifests a pleasure in darkness. He wil lnot come to the light lest his deeds should be reproved.

The nominal churches of this day are filled with fornication and adultery, the result of base, lustful passion, but these things, to a great extent, are kept covered. Ministers, in high places, are guilty, yet a cloak of godliness covers their dark deeds, and they pass on from year to year in their course of hypocrisy. Their sins have reached unto Heaven.

Fornication and adultery are estimated by many professing Christians as sins which God winketh at. These sins are practiced to a great extent. They do not acknowledge the claims of God's law upon them. They have broken the commandments of the great Jehovah, and are zealously teaching their hearers to do the same, declaring that the law of God is abolished, and consequently has no claims upon them. In accordance with this free state of things, sin does not appear so exceedingly sinful; for by the law is the knowledge of sin, We may expect to find men among those who thus teach, who will deceive, and lie, and give loose rein to lustful passions. But men and women who acknowledge the ten commandments binding, should carry out in their lives, the principles of all ten of the precepts given in awful grandeur from Sinai.

The Lord made this special covenant with ancient Israel: "Now, therefore, if ye will obey my voice indeed, and keep my covenant, then ye shall be a peculiar treasure unto me above all people; for all the earth is mine. And ye shall be unto me a kingdom of priests, and an holy nation." Ex. 19:5, 6. He addresses his commandment-keeping people in these last days, "But ye are a chosen generation, a royal priesthood, an holy nation, a peculiar people; that ye should show forth the praises of Him who hath called you out of darkness into his marvelous light." "Dearly beloved, I beseech you as strangers and pilgrims, abstain from fleshly lusts which war against the soul." 1 Pet. 2:9, 11.

But all who profess to keep the commandments of God are not possessing their bodies in sanctification and honor. They can have a powerful influence if they will be sanctified by the truths they profess. They profess to be standing upon the elevated platform of eternal truth, keeping all of God's commandments; therefore, if they indulge in sin, if they commit fornication and adultery, their crime is of tenfold greater magnitude than those I have referred to who do not acknowledge the law of God binding upon them. In a peculiar sense do those who profess to keep God's law dishonor him and reproach the truth by transgressing that law.

This very sin, fornication, prevailed among ancient Israel, which brought the signal manifestation of God's displeasure. The judgments of God followed close upon their heinous sin. Thousands of them fell, and their polluted bodies were left in the wilderness. "But with many of them God was not well pleased; for they were overthrown in the wilderness. Now these things were our examples, to the intent we should not lust after evil things, as they also lusted. Neither be ye idolaters, as were some of them; as it is written, The people sat down to eat and drink, and rose up to play. Neither let us commit fornication, as some of them committed, and fell in one day three and twenty thousand. Neither let us tempt Christ, as some of them also tempted, and were destroyed of serpents. Neither murmur ye, as some of them also murmured, and were destroyed of the destroyer. Now all these things happened unto them for ensamples; and they are written for our admonition, upon whom the ends of the world are come. Wherefore let him that thinketh he standeth, take heed lest he fall." 1 Cor. 10:5-12.

God's people, above all people in the world, should be patterns of piety, holy in heart and in conversation. The people whom God has chosen as his peculiar treasure, he requires to be elevated, refined, sanctified partakers of the divine nature, having escaped the corruption that is in the world through lust. If such indulge in sin and iniquity who make so high a profession, their guilt is very great, because they have great light, and have by their profession taken their position as God's special, chosen people, having the law of God written in their hearts. They signify their loyalty to the God of Heaven by yielding obedience to the laws of his government. They are God's representatives upon the earth. Any sin or transgression in them separates them from God, and, in a special manner, dishonors his name by giving the enemies of God's holy law occasion to reproach his cause and his people, whom he has called "a chosen generation, a royal priesthood, an holy nation, a peculiar people," that they should show forth the praises of Him that hath called them out of darkness into his marvelous light.

The people who are at war with the law of the great Jehovah, who consider it a special virtue to talk, and write, and act, the most bitter and hateful things, to show their contempt of that law, may make high and exalted profession of love to God, and apparently have much religious zeal, as did the Jewish chief priests and elders; yet in the day of God, "Found wanting" will be said to them by the Majesty of Heaven. By the law is the knowledge of sin. The mirror which discovers to them the defects in their character, they are infuriated against, because it points out their sins. Ministers who have rejected the light are fired with madness against God's holy law, as the Jewish priests were against the Son of God. They are in a terrible deception, deceiving souls, and being deceived themselves. They will not come to the light, lest their deeds should be reproved. Such will not be taught. But the people who profess to keep the law of God, he corrects, he reproves. He points out their sins, and lays open their iniquity; because he wishes to separate all sin and wickedness from them, that they may perfect holiness in his fear, and be prepared to die in the Lord, or to be translated to Heaven. God will rebuke, reprove, and correct them, that they may be refined, sanctified, elevated, and finally exalted to his throne.

The professed people of God are not all holy. Some are corrupt. God is seeking to elevate them; but these refuse to come up upon a high plane of action. The animal passions bear sway, and the moral and intellectual are overborne, and made servants to the animal. Those who do not control their passions cannot appreciate the atonement, or place a right value upon the worth of the soul. Salvation to them is not experienced nor understood. The gratification of their animal passions is to them the highest ambition of their lives. But nothing but purity and holiness will God accept. One spot, one wrinkle, one defect in the character, will debar them from Heaven, with all its glories and treasures, forever.

Ample provisions have been made for all who sincerely, earnestly, and thoughtfully, set about the work of perfecting holiness in the fear of God. Power and strength, grace and glory, have been provided through Christ, to be brought by ministering angels to the heirs of salvation. None are so low, and corrupt, and vile, but that they can find in Jesus, who died for them, strength, purity, and righteousness, if they will put away their sins, stop their course of iniquity, and turn with full purpose of heart to the living God. He is waiting to strip them of their garments, stained and polluted by sin, and to put upon them the pure robes of righteousness, and bid them live and not die. In him they may flourish. Their branches will not wither nor be fruitless. If they abide in him, they can draw sap and nourishment from him, be imbued with his Spirit, walk even as he walked, overcome as he overcame, and be exalted to his own right hand.

"Let not sin, therefore, reign in your mortal body, that ye should obey it, in the lust thereof. Neither yield ye your members as instruments of unrighteousness unto sin; but yield yourselves unto God as those that are alive from the dead, and your members as instruments of righteousness unto God." Rom. 6:12, 13. Professed Christians, if there is no further light given you than that contained in this text, you will be without excuse if you suffer yourselves to be controlled by base passions. The word of God is sufficient to enlighten the most beclouded mind. And it can be understood by those who have any wish to understand it. But notwithstanding all this, some of those who profess to make the word of God their study, are found living in direct opposition to its plainest teachings. But in order to leave men and women

A Solemn Appeal

without excuse, God has given plain and pointed testimonies, bringing them to the word they have neglected to follow. Yet all the light is turned from by those who serve their own lusts, and they will not cease their course of sin, but continue to take pleasure in unrighteousness, in the face of the threatenings and vengeance of God against those who do such things.

Chapter 4

Female Modesty

I have long been designing to speak to my sisters. They are not always careful to abstain from all appearance of evil. They are not all circumspect in their deportment, as becometh women professing godliness. Their words are not as select and well chosen as they should be for women who have received the grace of God. They are too familiar with their brethren. They linger around them, incline towards them, and seem to choose their society, and are highly gratified with their attention.

There is much jesting and joking and laughing indulged in by women professing godliness. This is all unbecoming, and grieves the Spirit of God. These exhibitions manifest a lack of true Christian refinement. These things indulged in do not strengthen the soul in God, but bring great darkness, drive the pure, refined, heavenly angels away, and bring those who engage in these wrongs down to a low level.

The sisters should encourage true meekness. They should not be forward, talkative, and bold, but modest and slow to speak. They should be courteous. To be kind, tender, pitiful, forgiving, and humble, would be becoming and well pleasing to God. If they occupy this position, they will not be burdened with undue attention from gentlemen. It will be felt by all that there is a sacred circle of purity around these God-fearing women, which shields them from any unwarrantable liberties. There is too much careless, loose, coarse freedom of manner by some women professing godliness, which leads to greater wrongs. Those godly women who occupy their minds and hearts in meditating upon themes which strengthen purity of life, which elevate the soul to commune with God, will not be easily led astray from the path of rectitude and virtue. They will be fortified against the sophistry of Satan, and prepared to withstand his seductive arts.

The fashion of the world, the desire of the eye, and the lust of the flesh, or vain glory, are connected with the fall of the unfortunate. That which is pleasing to the natural heart and carnal mind is cherished. If the lust of the flesh was rooted out of their hearts, they would not be so weak. If our sisters would feel the necessity of purifying their thoughts, and never suffer themselves to be careless in their deportment, which leads to improper acts, they would not be in danger of staining their purity. They would feel such an abhorrence of impure acts and deeds that they would not be found among the number who fall through the temptations of Satan, no matter who the medium might be whom Satan should select.

A preacher may deal in sacred, holy things, and yet not be holy in heart. He may give himself to Satan to work wickedness, and to corrupt the soul and body of his flock. Yet if the minds of women and youth professing to love and fear God were fortified with the Spirit of God; if they had trained their minds to purity of thought, and educated themselves to avoid all appearance of evil, they would be safe from any improper advances, and be secure from the prevailing corruption around them. The apostle has written concerning himself, "But I keep under my body, and bring it in subjection; lest that by any means, when I have preached to others, I myself should be a castaway." 1 Cor. 9:27.

If a minister of the gospel has not control of his lower passions; if he fails to follow the example of the apostle, and so dishonors his profession and faith as to even name the indulgence of sin, the sisters who profess godliness should not for an instant flatter themselves that sin and crime lose their sinfulness in the least because their minister dares to engage in them. Because men who are in responsible places show themselves to be familiar with sin, it should not lessen the guilt and enormity of the sin in the minds of any. Sin should appear just as sinful, just as abhorrent, as the word of God represents it to be, and the one who indulges in sin should, in the minds of the pure and elevated, be abhorred and withdrawn from, as they would flee from a serpent whose sting was deadly.

If the sisters were elevated, and possessed purity of heart, any corrupt advances, even from their minister, would be repulsed with such positiveness that they would never be repeated. Minds must be terribly befogged that can listen to the voice of the seducer because he is a minister, and therefore break God's plain and positive commands, and flatter themselves that they commit no sin. Have we not the words of John: "He that saith, I know him, and keepeth not his commandments, is a liar, and the truth is not in him"? What saith the law? "Thou shalt not commit adultery." The fact of a man's professing to keep God's holy law, and ministering in sacred things, should he take advantage of the confidence his position gives him to indulge his passions, should, of itself, be sufficient to lead any woman professing godliness, to see that, although his profession was as exalted as the heavens, any impure proposal coming from him was the work of Satan disguised as an angel of light. I cannot believe that the word of God is abiding in the hearts of those who are so readily controlled, and yield up their innocency and virtue upon the altar of lustful passion.

My sisters, you should avoid even the appearance of evil. In this fast age, which is reeking with corruption, you are not safe unless you stand guarded. Virtue and modesty are rare. I appeal to you as followers of Jesus Christ, making a high and exalted profession, to cherish this precious, priceless gem, modesty. This will guard virtue. If you have any hope of being finally exalted to join company with the pure, sinless angels, and live in an atmosphere where there is not the least taint of sin, cherish modesty and virtue. Nothing but purity, sacred purity, will abide the day of God, stand the grand review, and be received into a pure and holy Heaven.

The least insinuations, come from whatever source they may, inviting you to indulge in sin, or to allow the least unwarrantable liberty with your person, you should resent as the worst of insults to your dignified womanhood. The kiss upon your cheek, at an improper time and place, should lead you to repel the emissary of Satan with disgust. If it is from one in high places who is dealing in sacred things, the sin, in such a one, is of tenfold greater magnitude, and should lead a God-fearing woman or youth to recoil with horror, not only from the sin he would have you commit, but from the hypocrisy and villainy of one whom the people respect and honor as God's servant. In his ministry he is handling sacred things, yet hiding his baseness of heart under a ministerial cloak. Be afraid of anything like this familiarity. You may be sure that the least approach to it is the evidence of a lascivious mind and a lustful eye. If the least encouragement is given in this direction; if any of the liberties mentioned are tolerated, no better evidence can you give that your mind is not pure and chaste as it should be, and that sin and crime have charms for you. You lower the standard of your dignified, virtuous womanhood, and give unmistakable evidence that a low, brutal passion has been suffered to remain in your heart.

As I have seen the dangers of, and the sins among, those who profess better things—a class who are not suspected of being in any danger from these polluting sins—I have been led to inquire, Who, O Lord, shall stand when thou appearest? Only those who have clean hands and pure hearts shall abide the day of his coming.

I feel impelled by the Spirit of the Lord to urge my sisters who profess godliness to cherish modesty of deportment and a becoming reserve, with shamefacedness and sobriety. The liberties taken in this age of corruption should be no criterion for Christ's followers. These fashionable exhibitions of familiarity should not exist among Christians fitting for immortality. If lasciviousness, pollution, adultery, crime, and murder, are the order of the day among those who know not the truth, and who refuse to be controlled by the principles of God's word, how important that those who profess to be followers of Christ and closely allied to God and angels, should show them a better and nobler way. How important that their chastity and virtue stand in marked contrast with that of the class who are controlled by brute passions.

I have inquired, When will the youthful sisters act with propriety? But I know there will not be any decided change for the better until parents feel the importance of greater carefulness in educating their children correctly. They should teach them to act with reserve and modesty. They should educate them for usefulness, to be helps, to minister to others, rather than to be waited upon and ministered unto. Satan has the control of the minds of the youth generally. Fond parents, your daughters are not always taught self-denial and self-control. They are petted, and their pride is fostered. They are allowed to have their own way until they become headstrong and self-willed, and you are put to your wits' end to know what course to pursue, to save them from ruin. Satan is leading them on to be a proverb in the mouths of unbelievers, because of their boldness, their lack of reserve and want of female modesty.

The young boys are likewise left to have their own way.

They have scarcely entered their teens before they are by the side of little girls about their own age, accompanying them home, and making love to them. And the parents are so completely in bondage through their own indulgence, and their mistaken love for their children, that they dare not pursue a decided course to make a change, and restrain their too fast children.

With many young ladies, the boys is the theme of conversation, and with the young men, it is the girls. Out of the abundance of the heart the mouth speaketh. They talk of those subjects upon which their minds mostly run. The recording angel is writing the words of these professed Christian boys and girls. How will they be confused and ashamed when they meet them again in the day of God. There are too many children who are a sort of pious hypocrites. The youth who have not made a profession of religion stumble over these hypocritical ones, and are hardened against any effort that may be made by those interested in their salvation. Oh! that we could arouse fathers and mothers to have a sense of their duty. Oh! that they would feel deeply the weight of responsibility resting upon them. Then they might forestall the enemy, and gain precious victories for Jesus. Parents are not clear in this matter. They should investigate their lives closely, analyze their thoughts and motives, and see if they have been circumspect in their course of action. They should closely watch, to see if their example in conversation and deportment has been such as they would wish their children to imitate. Have purity and virtue shine out in your words and acts before your children.

There are families where the husband and father has not

preserved that reserve, that dignified, godlike manhood, which a follower of Jesus Christ should. He has failed to manifest kind, tender, courteous acts due to his wife, whom he has promised before God and angels to love and respect and honor while they both shall live. The girl employed to do the work may be free and somewhat forward in her attentions to dress his hair and be affectionately attentive, and he is pleased, foolishly pleased. And he is not as demonstrative in his attention and love as he once was to his wife. Be sure Satan is at work here. Respect your hired help, treat them kindly, considerately, but go no farther. Let your deportment be such that there will be no advances to familiarity from your help. If you have words of kindness and acts of courtesy to give, it is always safe to give them to your wife. It will be a great blessing to her, and will bring happiness to her heart which will be reflected back upon you again. Also, the wife may let her sympathies and interest and affection go out to another man beside her husband. He may be a member of the family, whom she makes a confidant, and to whom she relates her troubles, and, perhaps, her private family matters. She shows a preference for his society.

Satan is at the bottom of this; and unless she can be alarmed, and stopped just where she is, he will lead her to ruin. My sisters, you cannot observe too great caution in this matter. If you have tender, loving words and kindly attentions to bestow, let them be given him you have promised before God and angels to love, honor and respect, while you both shall live. Oh! how many lives are made bitter by the walls being broken down which inclose the privacies of every family, calculated to preserve purity and sanctity. A third person is taken into the confidence of the wife, and her private family matters are laid open before the special friend. This is the device of Satan to estrange the hearts of the husband and wife. Oh! that this would cease. What a world of trouble would be saved! Lock the faults of one another within your own hearts. Tell your troubles alone to God. He can give you right counsel and sure consolation, which will be pure, having no bitterness in it.

Chapter 5

Sentimentalism

I am acquainted with a number of cases where the women have thought their marriage a misfortune. They have read novels until their imaginations have become diseased, and they live in a world of their own creating. They think themselves women of sensitive minds, of superior, refined organizations. They think themselves great sufferers, martyrs, because they imagine their husbands are not so refined, not possessing such superior qualities that they can appreciate their own supposed virtue and refined organizations. These women have talked of this, and thought of it, until they are nearly maniacs upon this subject. They imagine their worth is superior to that of other mortals, and it is not agreeable to their fine sensibilities to associate with common humanity.

The women of this class have had their imaginations perverted by novel-reading, day-dreaming, and castle-building; by living in an imaginary world. They do not bring their ideas down to the common, useful duties of life. They do not take up the life-burdens which lie in their path, and seek to make happy, cheerful homes for their husbands. They lean upon them without so much as bearing their own burden. They expect others to anticipate their wants, and do for them, while they are at liberty to find fault and to question as they please. These women have a sort of love-sick sentimentalism, constantly thinking they are not appreciated; that their husbands do not give them all that attention they deserve. They imagine themselves martyrs.

The truth of the matter is this: if they would show themselves useful, their value might be appreciated; but when they pursue a course to constantly draw upon others for sympathy and attention, while they feel under no obligation to give the same in return, and pass along, reserved, cold, and unapproachable, bearing no burden for others, or feeling for their woes, there can be but little in their lives precious and valuable. These women have educated themselves to think that it has been a great condescension in them to marry the men they have; and therefore that their fine organizations will never be fully appreciated; and they act accordingly.

They view things altogether in a wrong light. They are unworthy of their husbands. They are a constant tax upon their care and patience, when, at the same time, they might be helps, lifting at the burdens of life with their husbands, instead of dreaming over unreal life found in novels and love romances. May the Lord pity the men who are bound to such useless machines, fit only to be waited upon, to eat, dress, and breathe.

These women who suppose they possess such sensitive, refined organizations make very useless wives and mothers. It is frequently the case that the affections are withdrawn from their husbands, who are useful, practical men; and they show much attention to other men, and with their love-sick sentimentalism draw upon the sympathies of others, tell them their trials, their troubles, their aspirations to do some high and elevated work, and reveal the fact that their married life is a disappointment, a hinderance to their doing the work they have anticipated they might do.

Oh! what wretchedness exists in families that might be happy. These women are a curse to themselves, and a curse to their husbands. In supposing themselves to be angels, they make themselves fools, and are nothing but heavy burdens. They leave right in their path, the common duties of life, which the Lord has left for them to do, and are restless and complaining, always looking for an easy, more exalted, and more agreeable work to do. Supposing themselves to be angels, they are found human after all. They are fretful, peevish, dissatisfied, jealous of their husbands because the larger portion of their time is not spent in waiting upon them. They complain of being neglected when their husbands are doing the very work they ought to do. Satan finds easy access to his class. They have no real love for any one but themselves. Yet Satan tells them that if such an one were their husband, they would be happy indeed. They are easy victims to the device of Satan, easy to be led to dishonor their own husbands, and to transgress the law of God.

I would say to women of this description, You can make your own happiness, or you can destroy it. You can make your position happy, or unbearable. The course you pursue will create happiness or misery for yourself. Have these never thought that their husbands must tire of them in their uselessness, in their peevishness, in their fault-finding, in their passionate fits of weeping, while imagining their case so pitiful? Their irritable, peevish disposition is indeed weaning the affections of their husbands from them, and driving them to seek for sympathy, and peace, and comfort, elsewhere than at home. A poisonous atmosphere is in their dwelling. And home is anything but a place of rest, or peace and happiness to them. The husband is subject to Satan's temptation, and his affections are placed on forbidden objects, and he is lured on to crime, and finally lost.

Great is the work and mission of women especially of those who are wives and mothers. They can be a blessing to all around them. They can have a powerful influence for good. Woman may have a transforming influence if she will only consent to yield her way and her will to God, and let him control her mind, affections, and being. She can have an influence which will tend to refine and elevate those with whom she associates. But she is generally unconscious of the power she possesses. She exerts an unconscious influence. It seems to work out naturally from a sanctified life, a renewed heart. It is the fruit that grows naturally upon the good tree of divine planting. Self is forgotten and immerged in the life of Christ. To be rich in good works comes as naturally as her breath. She lives to do others good, and yet is ready to say, I am an unprofitable servant.

God has assigned woman her mission, and if she, in her humble way, to the best of her ability, makes a heaven of her home, faithfully and lovingly performing her home-duties to her husband and children, continually seeking to let a holy light shine from her useful, pure, and virtuous life, to brighten all around her, she is doing the work left her of the Master, and will hear from his divine lips, "Well done, good and faithful servant, enter thou into the joy of thy Lord." These women who are doing what their hands find to do with ready willingness, and with cheerfulness of spirit, aiding their husbands to bear their burdens, and training their children for God, are missionaries in the highest sense. They are engaged in an important branch of the great work to be done on earth to prepare mortals for a higher life. They will receive their reward. Children are to be trained for Heaven, and fitted to shine in the courts of the Lord's kingdom. When parents, especially mothers, have a true sense of the responsible work God has left for them to do, they will not be so much engaged in the business which concerns their neighbors, with which they have nothing to do. They will not engage in the fashionable gossip from house to house, dwelling upon the faults and inconsistencies of their neighbors. They will feel so great a burden of care for their own children that they can find no time to take up a reproach against their neighbor. Gossipers and news-carriers are a terrible curse to neighborhoods and church es. Two-thirds of all the church trials arise from this source.

God requires all to do the duties of to-day with faithfulness. This is much neglected by the larger share of professed Christians. Especially is present duty lost sight of by the class I have mentioned, who imagine that they are of a higher order of beings than their fellow-mortals around them. The fact of their minds' turning in this channel, is proof that they are of an inferior order, narrow, conceited, and selfish. They feel high above the lowly and humble poor. Such, Jesus says he has called. They are forever trying to secure position, to gain applause, to obtain credit for doing a work that others cannot do, some great work. But it disturbs the fine grain of their refined organism to associate with the humble and unfortunate. They mistake the reason altogether. The reason they shun any of these duties not so agreeable, is because of their supreme selfishness. Dear self is the center of all their actions and motives.

The Majesty of Heaven, whom angels worshiped, who was rich in honor, splendor, and glory, came to the earth, and when he found himself in fashion as a man, he did not plead his refined nature as an excuse to hold himself aloof from the unfortunate. He was found in his work among the afflicted, the poor, distressed, and needy ones. Christ was the embodiment of refinement and purity. His was an exalted life and character, yet he was found in his labor, not among men of high-sounding titles, not among the most honorable of this world, but with the despised and needy. "I came," says the divine Teacher, "to save that which was lost." Yes, the Majesty of Heaven was ever found working to help those who most needed help. May the example of Christ put to shame the excuses of that class who are so attracted to their poor self that they consider it beneath their refined taste and their high calling to help the most helpless. Such have taken a position higher than their Lord, and in the end will be astonished to find themselves even lower than that class, to mingle with, and to work for whom, shocked their refined, sensitive natures. True, it may not always be agreeable or pleasant to unite with the Master and be co-workers with him in helping the very class who stand most in need of help. But this is the work Christ humbled himself to do. Is the servant greater than his Lord? He has given the example, and enjoins upon us to copy it. It may be disagreeable, yet duty demands that just such a work be performed.

I have felt deeply as I have seen the powerful influence animal passions have had in controlling men and women of no ordinary intelligence and ability. They are capable of engaging in a good work, of exerting a powerful influence, were they not enslaved by base passions. They have listened to the most solemn, impressive discourses upon the judgment, which seemed to bring them before the tribunal of God, causing them to fear and quake, yet an hour would hardly elapse before they have been engaged in their favorite, bewitching sin, polluting their own bodies. They were such slaves to this awful crime that they seemed devoid of power to control their passions. We have labored for some earnestly; we have entreated, we have wept and prayed over them, yet we have known that right amid all our earnest effort and distress, the force of sinful habit has obtained the mastery. These sins would be committed. The consciences of some of the guilty, through severe attacks of sickness, or by being powerfully convicted, have been aroused, and have so scourged them, that it has led to confession of these things, with deep humiliation. Others are alike guilty. They have practiced this sin

nearly their whole lifetime, and with their broken-down constitutions, and, with their sieve-like memories, are reaping the result of this pernicious habit, yet are too proud to confess. They
are secretive, and have not shown compunctions of conscience
for this great sin and wickedness. They seem to be insensible to
the influence of the Spirit of God. The sacred and common are
alike to them. The common practice of a vice so degrading as
polluting their own bodies has not led to bitter tears and heartfelt
repentance. They feel that their sin is against themselves alone.
Here they mistake. Are they diseased in body or mind, others are
made to feel. Others suffer. Mistakes are made. The memory is
deficient. The imagination is at fault. And there is a deficiency
everywhere which seriously affects those with whom they live,
and who associate with them. These feel mortification and regret
because these things are known by another.

I have mentioned these cases to illustrate the power of this
soul-and-body-destroying vice. The entire mind is given up to
low passion. The moral and intellectual are over- borne by the
baser powers. The body is enervated, the brain is weakened. The
material there deposited to nourish the system is squandered.
The drain upon the system is great. The fine nerves of the brain,
by being excited to unnatural action, become benumbed and
in a measure paralyzed. The moral and intellectual are growing weaker, while the animal passions are growing stronger, and
being more largely developed by exercise. The appetite for unhealthful food clamors for indulgence. It is impossible to fully
arouse the moral sensibilities of those persons who are addicted

to the habit of self-abuse, to appreciate eternal things. You cannot lead such to delight in spiritual exercises. Impure thoughts seize and control the imagination, fascinate the mind, and next follows an almost uncontrollable desire for impure acts. If the mind were educated to contemplate elevating subjects, the imagination trained to reflect upon pure and holy things, it would be fortified against this terrible, debasing, soul-and-body-destroying indulgence. It would become accustomed to linger with delight upon the high, the heavenly, the pure, and the sacred, and could not be attracted to this base, corrupt, and vile indulgence.

What can we say of those who are living right in the blazing light of truth, yet daily practicing and following in a course of sin and crime. Forbidden, exciting pleasures have a charm for them, and hold and control their entire being. Such take pleasure in unrighteousness and iniquity, and must perish outside of the city of God, with every abominable thing.

I have sought to arouse parents to their duty, yet they sleep on. Your children practice secret vice, and they deceive you. You have such implicit confidence in them, that you think them too good and innocent to be capable of secretly practicing iniquity. Parents fondle and pet their children, and indulge them in pride, but do not restrain them with firmness and decision. They are so much afraid of their willful, stubborn spirits, that they fear to come in contact with them; but the sin of negligence, which was marked against Eli, will be their sin. The exhortation of Peter is of the highest value to all who are striving for immortality. Those of like precious faith are addressed:

"Simon Peter, a servant and an apostle of Jesus Christ, to them that have obtained like precious faith with us through the righteousness of God and our Saviour Jesus Christ: Grace and peace be multiplied unto you through the knowledge of God, and of Jesus our Lord, according as his divine power hath given unto us all things that pertain unto life and godliness, through the knowledge of Him that hath called us to glory and virtue: whereby are given unto us exceeding great and precious promises; that by these ye might be partakers of the divine nature, having escaped the corruption that is in the world through lust. And besides this, giving all diligence, add to your faith, virtue; and to virtue, knowledge; and to knowledge, temperance; and to temperance, patience; and to patience, godliness; and to godliness, brotherly kindness; and to brotherly kindness, charity. For if these things be in you, and abound, they make you that ye shall neither be barren nor unfruitful in the knowledge of our Lord Jesus Christ. But he that lacketh these things is blind, and cannot see afar off, and hath forgotten that he was purged from his old sins. Wherefore the rather, brethren, give diligence to make your calling and election sure: for if ye do these things, ye shall never fall: for so an entrance shall be ministered unto you abundantly into the everlasting kingdom of our Lord and Saviour Jesus Christ." 2 Pet. 1:1-11.

We are in a world where light and knowledge abound; yet many, claiming to be of like precious faith, are willingly ignorant. Light is all around them; yet they do not appropriate it to themselves. Parents do not see the necessity of informing them-

83

selves, of obtaining knowledge, and putting that knowledge to a practical use in their married life. If they followed out the exhortation of the apostle, and lived upon the plan of addition, they would not be unfruitful in the knowledge of our Lord Jesus Christ. Many do not understand the work of sanctification. It is a progressive work. It is not attained to in an hour or a day, and then maintained without any special effort on their part. Many seem to think they have attained to it when they have only learned the first lessons in addition.

Many parents do not obtain the knowledge that they should respecting the married life. They are not guarded lest Satan take advantage of them, and control their minds and their lives. They do not see that God requires them to control their married lives from any excesses. But very few feel it to be a religious duty to govern their passions. They have united themselves in marriage to the object of their choice, and therefore reason that marriage sanctifies the indulgence of the baser passions. Even men and women professing godliness give loose rein to their lustful passions, and have no thought that God holds them accountable for the expenditure of vital energy, which weakens their hold on life and enervates the entire system.

The marriage covenant covers sins of the darkest hue. Some men and women professing godliness debase their own bodies through the indulgence of the corrupt passions, which lowers them beneath the brute creation. They abuse the powers God has given them to be preserved in sanctification and honor. Health and life are sacrificed upon the altar of base passion. The higher, nobler powers are brought into subjection to the animal propensities. Those who thus sin are not acquainted with the result of their course. Could all see the amount of suffering they bring upon themselves by their own wrong and sinful indulgence, they would be alarmed. Some, at least, would shun the course of sin which brings such dreaded wages. A miserable existence is entailed upon so large a class that death to them would be preferable to life; and many do die prematurely, their lives being sacrificed in the inglorious work of excessive indulgence of the animal passions. Because they are married, they think they commit no sin.

These men and women will one day learn what lust is, and behold the result of its gratification. Passion may be found of as base a quality in the marriage relation as outside of it. The apostle Paul exhorts husbands to love their wives "even as Christ also loved the church, and gave himself for it." "So ought men to love their wives as their own bodies. He that loveth his wife loveth himself. For no man ever yet hated his own flesh; but nourisheth and cherisheth it, even as the Lord the church." Eph. 5:25, 28, 29. It is not pure love which actuates a man to make his wife an instrument to administer to his lust. It is the animal passions which clamor for indulgence. How few men show their love in the manner specified by the apostle: "Even as Christ also loved the church, and gave himself for it, that he might [not pollute it, but] sanctify and cleanse it," "that it should be holy and without blemish." This is the quality of love in the married relation which God recognizes as holy. Love is a pure and holy principle. Lustful passion will not admit of restraint, and will not be dictated or controlled by reason. It is blind to consequences. It will not reason from cause to effect. Many women are suffering from great debility, and with settled disease, brought upon them because the laws of their being have not been regarded. Nature's laws have been trampled upon. The brain nerve-power is squandered by men and women because called into unnatural action to gratify base passions; and this hideous monster, base, low passion; assumes the delicate name of love.

Many professed Christians are more animal than divine. They are, in fact, about all animal. A man of this type degrades the wife he has promised to nourish and cherish. She is made by him an instrument to minister to the gratification of his low, lustful propensities. Very many women submit to become slaves to lustful passion. They do not possess their bodies in sanctification and honor. The wife does not retain the dignity and self- respect she possessed previous to marriage. This holy institution should have preserved and increased her womanly respect and holy dignity. Her chaste, dignified, godlike womanhood, has been consumed upon the altar of base passion. It has been sacrificed to please her husband. She soon loses respect for her husband, who does not regard the laws to which the brute creation yields obedience. The married life become a galling yoke; for love dies out, and, frequently, distrust, jealousy, and hate, take its place.

No man can truly love his wife if she will patiently submit to become his slave, and minister to his degraded passions. She loses, in her passive submission, the value she once possessed in his eyes. He sees her dragged down from everything elevating, to a low level, and soon he suspects that she will, perhaps, as tamely submit to be degraded by another as by himself. He doubts her constancy and purity, tires of her, and seeks new objects which will arouse and intensify his hellish passions. The law of God is not regarded. These men are worse than brutes. They are demons in human form. They are unacquainted with the elevating, ennobling principles of true, of sanctified, love.

The wife becomes jealous of the husband. She suspects that he will just as readily pay his addresses to another as to her, if opportunity should offer. She sees that he is not controlled by conscience, nor the fear of God. All these sanctified barriers are broken down by lustful passions. All that is godlike in the husband is made the servant of low, brutish lust.

The world is filled with men and women of this order; and neat, tasty, yea, expensive houses contain a hell within. Imagine, if you can, what the offspring of such parents must be. Will not the children sink lower in the scale than their parents? Parents give the stamp of character to their children. Children that are born of these parents inherit qualities of mind from them which are of a low and base order. Satan nourishes anything tending to corruption. The matter now to be settled is, shall the wife feel bound to yield implicitly to the demands of her husband when she sees that nothing but base passions control him, and when her reason and knowledge are convinced that she does it to the injury of her body, which God has enjoined upon her to possess in sanctification and honor, and to preserve a living sacrifice to

God?

It is not pure, holy love which leads the wife to gratify the animal propensities of her husband at the expense of health and life. If she possesses true love and wisdom, she will seek to divert the mind of her husband from the gratification of lustful passions, to high and spiritual themes, dwelling upon interesting spiritual subjects. It may be necessary to humbly and affectionately urge, even at the risk of his displeasure, that she cannot debase her body by yielding to sexual excess. She should, in a tender, kind manner, remind him that God has the first and highest claim upon her entire being, which claim she cannot disregard, for she will be held accountable in the great day of God. "What! know ye not that your body is the temple of the Holy Ghost which is in you, which ye have of God, and ye are not your own? for ye are bought with a price; therefore glorify God in your body, and in your spirit, which are God's." 1 Cor. 6:19, 20. "Ye are bought with a price; be not ye the servants of men." 1 Cor. 7:23.

Woman can do much, if she will, through her judicious influence, by elevating her affections, and in sanctification and honor preserving her refined, womanly dignity. In thus doing, she can save her husband and herself, thus performing a double work, and fulfilling her high mission, sanctifying her husband by her influence. In this delicate, difficult matter to manage, much wisdom and patience are necessary, as well as moral courage and fortitude. Strength and grace can be found in prayer. Sincere love is to be the ruling principle of the heart. Love to God and love to your husband can be the only right ground of action.

Let the woman decide that it is the husband's prerogative to have full control of her body, and to mold her mind to suit his in every respect, and run in the same channel of his own, and she yields her individuality. Her identity is lost, submerged in that of her husband. She is a mere machine for him to move and control, a creature of his will and pleasure. He thinks for her, decides for her, and acts for her. She dishonors God in this passive position. She has a responsibility before God which it is her duty to preserve.

When the wife yields her body and mind to the control of her husband, being passive to his will in all things, sacrificing her conscience, her dignity, and even her identity, she loses the opportunity of exerting that mighty influence for good which she should possess to elevate her husband. She could soften his stern nature, and her sanctifying influence could be exerted in a manner to refine, purify, and lead him to strive earnestly to govern his passions, and be more spiritually minded, that they might be partakers together of the divine nature, having escaped the corruption that is in the world through lust. The power of influence can be great to lead the mind to high and noble themes, above the low, sensual indulgences which the heart unrenewed by grace naturally seeks. If the wife feels that she must, in order to please her husband, come down to his standard, when animal passion is the principal basis of his love, controlling his actions, she displeases God; for she fails to exert a sanctifying influence upon her husband. If she feels that she must submit to the animal passions of her husband without a word of remonstrance, she does not understand her duty to him, nor to her God. Sexual excess will effectually destroy a love for devotional exercises, will take from the brain the substance needed to nourish the system, and will most effectually exhaust the vitality. No woman should aid her husband in this work of self-destruction. She will not do it if she is enlightened, and truly loves her husband.

The more the animal passions are indulged and exercised, the stronger do they become, and the more violent will be their clamors for indulgence. Let God-fearing men and women awake to their duty. Many professing Christianity are suffering with paralysis of nerve and brain because of their intemperance in this direction. Rottenness is in the bones and marrow of many who are regarded as good men, who pray and weep, and who stand in high places, but whose polluted carcasses will never pass the portals of the heavenly city. Oh! that I could make all understand their obligations to God to preserve the mental and physical organism in the best condition to render perfect service to God.

Let the Christian wife refrain, both in word and act, from exciting the animal passions of her husband. Many have no strength at all to waste in this direction. They have already, from their youth up, weakened their brains, and sapped their constitutions, by the gratification of their animal passions. Self-denial and temperance should be the watch-word in married life; then, when children are born to parents, they will not be so liable to have the moral and intellectual organs weak, and the animal strong. Vice in children is almost universal. Is there not a cause?

Who have given them the stamp of character?

The mind of a man or woman does not come down in a moment from purity and holiness, to depravity, corruption, and crime. It takes time to transform the human to the divine, or to degrade those formed in the image of God, to brutes, or to the satanic. By beholding, we become changed. Man, formed in the image of his Maker, can so educate his mind that sin which he once loathed, will become pleasant to him. As he ceases to watch and pray, he ceases to guard the citadel, the heart, and engages in sin and crime. The mind is debased, and it is impossible to elevate it from corruption while it is being educated to enslave the moral and intellectual powers, and bring them in subjection to the grosser passions. It is constant war against the carnal mind, aided by the refining influence of the grace of God, which will attract it upward, and habituate it to meditate upon pure and holy things.

Many children are born with the animal passions largely in the ascendency, while the moral and intellectual are but feebly developed. These children need the most careful culture to bring out, strengthen and develop the moral and intellectual, and have these take the lead. Children are not trained for God. Their moral and religious education is neglected. The animal passions are being constantly strengthened, while the moral faculties are becoming enfeebled.

Some children begin to excite their animal passions in their infancy; and, as they increase in years, the lustful passions grow with their growth, and strengthen with their strength. Their minds are not at rest. Girls desire the society of boys; and boys, that of the girls. Their deportment is not reserved and modest. They are bold and forward, taking indecent liberties. Their corrupt habits of self-abuse have debased their minds, and tainted their souls. Vile thoughts, novel-reading, low books, and love-stories, excite the imagination, and just suit their depraved minds. They do not love work. They complain of fatigue when engaged in labor. Their backs ache. Their heads ache. Is there not sufficient cause? Are they fatigued because of their labor? No. Yet their parents indulge them in their complaints, and release them from labor and responsibility. This is the very worst thing they can do for them. They are removing almost the only barrier to Satan's having free access to their weakened minds. Useful labor would be a safeguard in some measure from his decided control of them.

The corrupting doctrine which has prevailed, that, as viewed from a health standpoint, the sexes must mingle together, has done its mischievous work. When parents and guardians manifest one tithe of the shrewdness which Satan possesses, then can this associating of sexes be nearer harmless. As it is, Satan is most successful in his efforts to bewitch the minds of the youth; and the mingling of boys and girls only increases the evil twentyfold. Let boys and girls be kept employed in useful labor. If they are tired, they will have less inclination to corrupt their own bodies.

We invite you to view the complete
selection of titles we publish at:

www.TEACHServices.com

or write or email us your praises,
reactions, or thoughts about this
or any other book we publish at:

TEACH Services, Inc.
P.O. Box 954
Ringgold, GA 30736

info@TEACHServices.com

Finally, if you are interested in seeing
your own book in print, please contact us at

publishing@teachservices.com.

We would be happy to review your manuscript for free.